Vietnam: The Last Combat Marines

Vietnam: The Last Combat Marines

Military and Political Times of the Baby Boomer War

David Gerhardt

ISBN: 978-0-692-13026-1

This is a work of nonfiction.

Vietnam: The Last Combat Marines

In 1970–71, the United States was deescalating its involvement in the Vietnam War, but the military commanders continued to push engagement with the enemy. It was a time of uncertainty for the soldiers. Similar to the populace in the United States, troops were divided politically and emotionally as they faced death or injury from booby traps, snipers, ambushes, and even friendly fire. On May 7, 1971, the Second Battalion, First Marine Regiment, First Marine Division, ceased combat operations and pulled its fighting forces to the rear to stand down for redeployment to the States. Fox Company became the final rifle company to leave the field, and its soldiers became the US Marine Corps' last ground-combat marines.

This is a story based on real-life experiences and is a product of decades of sleepless nights and early mornings, when unsolicited memories forced me to relive and analyze one of my life's most memorable years.

Semper fi,

Dave Gerhardt

I dedicate this memoir, with all my love, to my sons, Brandon and Adam, with whom I have been so blessed, along with the additional blessings of my dear daughters-in-law, Tina and Kelly, and to my very precious grandchildren, Wesley, Morgan, and Emily, (plus one on the way), who make my life complete.

In loving memory of my parents,

Charles and Jeanne Gerhardt

They courageously endured the daily agony of having a son leave home to fight in a war.

Contents

Preface

Our Home in Groveport, Ohio

There is a popular saying among soldiers and their families: "It is easier to go to war than to send to war." It was many years after I returned home that my mother opened up about Vietnam and "that horrible year" her eldest son was deployed there. She told me that she cried herself to sleep every night. These words still cause me to tear up. For me, it was a young man's journey. I was there to live out my childhood fantasy—that of wanting to be like Sergeant Saunders of the 1960s World War II weekly TV series, *Combat!*[1]

Vietnam was hot, humid, and uncomfortable. The mosquitoes had a picnic every night, and I was both their dinner and dessert. The firefights, enemy snipers, rocket attacks, and booby traps made days and nights dangerous, and sometimes terrifying. Many of the killed and wounded soldiers were comrades in my respective units. It was nothing like the TV series *Combat!* —there was no glamour, and there were no idols. A firefight with the enemy was frightening, not exciting. Death was real, and so was that hollow and helpless feeling of sorrow that came afterward. The blood and guts were genuine and not Hollywood props.

I now have two sons. I cannot imagine how I would feel if one of them was sent into a war zone. It would be ten times more difficult worrying about them as a parent than it was for me to live through it as a young adult. While I was there, knowing I was okay, my mother and father were watching nightly news reports showing actual video of battles and medevacs of our soldiers and listening to those dreadful weekly numbers of dead, wounded, and missing Americans. "There were 209 American soldiers killed in Vietnam this week, 442 injured, and 2 missing in action," the news anchor would stoically report. This dreaded weekly accounting instilled fear into all parents, spouses, relatives, and friends of loved ones serving in this Southeast Asian hellhole. My mother would whisper to herself, "Could one of those be David?" and then tearfully pray for my safety.

The true heroes of this war were those who died or were seriously injured, our brothers who are missing in action, those who were prisoners of war, the Gold Star spouses, parents, and relatives, and all the loved ones of those who were there. My wonderful mother and father, along with the parents of many of my Vietnam brothers and sisters, are no longer with us. They endured a lot during their lives, including the Great Depression, World War II, and sending a son or daughter, or multiple children, to Vietnam.

May God please bless our parents.

Part I

★★★

1.1. Brainwashed

"Your Marine Corps profession is *killer*," bellowed my class instructor. "Communism wants to destroy your democracy. You will be counted on, like so many brave warriors before you, to defend our red, white, and blue with honor. Kill as many of those Communist bastards as possible because that will be your job. You are going to be a professional killer with a license to hunt Commie gooks in Vietnam!"

Classes in boot camp were informative and motivational, and they typically consisted of an entire company comprising approximately 280 men. We had nearly eighty hours of classroom instruction. The most memorable classes included: personal hygiene, Geneva Convention guidelines including prisoner-of-war requirements (a prisoner must give only his name, rank, serial number, and age), first aid, weapons knowledge (both ours and the enemy's) including how to fix a jam if an M16 did not fire, mines, a one-hour class on "how to recognize a homosexual," the history of the Marine Corps and heroic battles, a nuclear-warfare class, jungle survival and rescue instructions, venereal diseases, Vietnam (including weather, terrain, enemy tactics, malaria, snakes, etc.), the respect and treatment of prisoners, local citizens, dead enemy soldiers, farm animals, and pets, the threat that communism posed to the existence of the free world, and the Uniform Code of Military Justice including serious wartime violations that could result in "your ugly mug hanging from a rope."

Notes: A partial list of capital crimes included the wartime crimes of desertion, espionage, disobeying a superior officer's order, and mutiny, as well as the wartime or peacetime crimes of murder and rape.

Military executions between 1942 and 1961 (the last execution) totaled 160 soldiers, mostly by hanging but some by firing squad.[2]

I remember one very passionate class instructor who lectured us on the Marine Corps and its motto, Semper Fidelis. Its meaning was "always faithful"—faithful to yourself, your comrades, your corps, your country, and your God. I became proud of my new occupation and employer.

Classes were a welcome respite from physical training or marching in the blistering sun on steamy hot pavement. Many of the class instructors were loud and intimidating, but they were dedicated and good teachers. Some would begin with a filthy joke, and others would begin with a threat: "I'd love to catch just one of you maggots sleeping in my class." I found the classes interesting and informative and the jokes funny although I sometimes fought to stay awake. Learning what was taught was up to the individual; there were no tests on most lessons, but I took detailed notes in every class. I felt that most sessions were worthwhile and potential lifesavers once I moved on to Vietnam. I would later find this to be true, especially in the early months of my deployment when training substituted for a lack of combat experience.

At nineteen years and six months, I entered the marines as one of the older of the seventy to eighty recruits in my platoon. The youngest were seventeen-year-old boys. We were naïve and believed ourselves to be invincible. The drill instructors and class instructors manipulated our emotions into hatred for our country's enemies. By the end of boot camp, Infantry Training Regiment, Scout Sniper School, and basic infantry training, I was eager to go kill those hated "Commie gooks." The marines called this being gung ho. Oorah!

Unfortunately for my new fervent attitude, the United States had begun to scale down our operations in Vietnam, and I was assigned permanent stateside duty at Camp Pendleton, California. I was a poor stateside marine and failed to be promoted during my initial nine-month stay, all the while watching most of my comrades ascend to private first class (E-2), and some even further, to lance corporal (E-3). I took a lot of razzing from my peers for my low rank.

We spent most of our time rehearsing riot duty as we trained to battle hippies in San Francisco and intervene in race riots in the Watts section of Los Angeles. Riot training consisted of mounting a bayonet to our M14 rifles, putting on our gas masks, and, in synchronized fashion, stomping loudly and slowly forward, shoulder to shoulder. The noise, the sheer number of us with nonhuman-looking heads, and bayonets with six-and-three-quarters-inch blades attached to our rifles were supposed to intimidate rioters to back away. We were told that, if deployed, only noncommissioned officers (E-4 and higher) would be issued bullets unless our lives were in imminent danger.

Full days of stomping on steamy hot pavement, in the hot California sun, with my face covered by a gas mask, was miserable duty. My feet would eventually feel like they were on fire and perspiration would run down my sweltering body from underneath my gas mask. And it was boring! Fortunately, I was standing in formation on one blessed early morning when our platoon sergeant asked for forty volunteers to go to Vietnam. I received (and mostly ignored) a lot of good advice from relatives and friends prior to leaving for the military. The one that I heard most often was “Never volunteer” (another was “Keep your head down”).

I left California three weeks later as a private (E-1), the same rank I had when I enlisted and the lowest of all positions in the armed forces. My one-year journey into an unknown realm was just beginning. It was a journey that would immerse me into a death-defying theater of war. One in which I would wear many hats: starting my deployment as a combat grenadier; being reassigned as an awards writer for the wounded, the heroic, and brothers who did not make it back alive; and finally becoming a combat squad leader. In this relatively short period of my life, I would travel the infamous Ho Chi Minh Trail, camp in jungles, mountains, and rice paddies, interact with the Vietnamese people, engage in firefights with the enemy, and experience sorrow as I had never known before.

I would acclimate well to a war zone and would return to California a year later as a sergeant (E-5), at least one rank higher than my peers who had remained stateside. However, at this point in my pre-Vietnam days, rank was not of utmost importance. From my early Sunday school classes to my latter church years, my favorite hymn was "Onward Christian Soldiers." I always imagined myself doing as the lyrics seemed to be directing me, "marching as to war."[3]

1.2. Arrival in Vietnam

After a brief four-to-five-day staging time in Okinawa, we "volunteers" boarded a C-130 cargo plane for Vietnam. Actually, only about five of us had volunteered; the other thirty-five had been "volunteered." A salty staff sergeant (E-6) who was on the plane told us to sit on our helmets so that "if enemy fire comes up through the plane, it won't blow your balls off." About half of us thought this was funny, but most of us sat on our helmets anyway, including me. After a short, noisy flight, we landed at the Da Nang airbase in South Vietnam. The salty staff sergeant was the first to sarcastically say, "Welcome to Vietnam."

As I exited the plane, the first thing I noticed was that the humidity was as high as it was in Okinawa. My time in Okinawa had not been enough to acclimate me to the drenching heat and humidity. We grabbed our sea bags and followed instructions given to us by another staff sergeant to "load up." Two cattle trucks transported us from the Da Nang airbase to Camp Lauer, our new marine base camp. They were nicknamed cattle trucks because of their wide-open beds with side railings. I climbed into the crowded bed in the first truck. Our route took us through a part of Da Nang, South Vietnam's second-largest city.

There was a well-known saying we used when playing sports in school: "Sometimes it's better to be lucky than good." I did not expect to need Lady Luck on a simple drive from the Da Nang airbase to our base camp, but I quickly realized the value of being "lucky" in a war zone. It turned out that I was fortunate to jump on the first truck. The second truck got its tires shot out by local Vietnamese policemen with US-issued M16 rifles. I heard the shots and later got a firsthand report from a still-shaky and pale-faced buddy who was one of the cows on the second truck. The driver hit a local family on a motor scooter. Scooters were a common method of transportation, and many families would load the family scooter with the husband (driver), wife, and all the children (up to about a dozen).

The driver briefly stopped and then attempted to continue toward our base. In Vietnam, the largest vehicles on the road prevailed over local traffic laws. This was especially true with Vietnamese drivers (driving our trucks), but it also happened with American drivers. The roads in Da Nang were always busy, and it was the responsibility of smaller vehicles and pedestrians to stay out of the way of the bigger bullies. Additionally, the drivers of all vehicles seemed to always be in a hurry, and the locals on scooters were very aggressive, darting in and out of traffic and around the trucks, making it difficult for the truck drivers to see smaller scooters in time to safely avoid squishing them.

Vietnamese civilians blamed American drivers for all the accidents and injuries whenever we were involved, and they pressured the police to hold Americans accountable. My buddy said that he was sitting with the other marines in the back of truck number two while shots were fired just a few feet below them. They heard about a dozen rounds and also the pops from the tires bursting. The marines had no idea what was going on, and many thought the Viet Cong (VC) were attacking them. Had they been issued weapons upon exiting their plane, there would have likely been a firefight right there on the streets of Da Nang between two "friendly" forces. Once the reason for the police action became clear, they were nervous and afraid that the local police were going to blame all of them for the accident and execute them on the spot. At one point, one of the policemen aimed his M16 at the back of the truck and instructed them to all get out. Some of the marines whispered about making a break for it, but they were surrounded. They were taken down the road and told to sit. My buddy thought this was going to be it. Eventually (about an hour later), another truck came and transported them to our base. The truck driver was not allowed to leave, and no one knew what happened to him.

The entire incident was surreal, as if we were a part of the opening act of a play. It was attention grabbing; a quick realization that our friends were not always friendly. I did not dwell on it. It was time to get my rifle and ammo and be assigned to my unit. Time to kill some gooks!

Notes: I learned later in my tour that the United States paid a salarium to the victims and their families for accidental injuries and deaths. Also, we began to require driver-safety classes for American jeep and truck drivers.

The word gook was used to refer to our enemy. The rest of the indigenous people were called villagers, natives, women, children; we meant no disrespect with slang terms such as mama-san, papa-san, baby-san, and other names.

On my first night in Vietnam, I slept on a cot in a barrack at Camp Lauer. I awoke the following morning with a feeling like I was on another planet, which could be descriptive of any war zone. There were sandbags surrounding our base perimeter and bunkers throughout the compound. Multiple layers of razor wire and two- or three-story towers further protected us. Everyone traveled with a weapon, even if only going to the outdoor bathrooms. It was as if I had landed on Mars and now had to protect myself from the Martians. I soon understood why American soldiers referred to the United States as the "world."

1.3. The Bloop Man

On my fourth day in Vietnam, I received my gear that I was going to need in the field, an M16 with magazines and ammo, and I was in a helicopter heading for the bush. I remember looking out the side door of the chopper at the rice paddies and seeing the people with umbrella straw hats working in them, water buffaloes (my first exposure to them), a nearby mountain, and even an ocean beach (later identified as China Beach). We landed in a rice paddy somewhere in South Vietnam. I had no idea where I was and was greeted by a corporal who said he was my squad leader. He seemed glad to have me as well as another marine who had been on the same chopper.

I was soon informed that we were replacements for two marines who had drowned in a nearby river while attempting to swim after the bodies of two VC soldiers that the squad had shot off a raft in the middle of the night. The squad members were exceedingly upset with our company commander. When the squad leader called in the kills, the company commander had replied, “Get those bodies.” Confirmed kills were trophies to some leaders because they boosted the weekly enemy body count.

Naturally, the marines’ deaths were very personal to all the guys in my new unit. They had witnessed the unnecessary fatalities of two brothers. The squad leader was a good swimmer and he had dived into the river to try to save his men, but the current was too strong, and he was lucky to make it back to shore himself. The two marines were found downstream the following morning. There were no VC found, but it was customary for them to recover their own.

On the second day in my new unit, my squad leader took away my M16 and handed me an M79 grenade launcher, a vest full of M79 grenades, and a Colt .45-caliber pistol in a holster with loaded magazines. “One of the men we lost was our bloop man,” he said.

All infantry marines were required to fire the M79 grenade launcher in training, and, like most everyone else, I had fired one round, which prepared me as a combat grenadier—I guess. I put on the vest, which had little pouches on the entire front and sides—top to bottom and side to side. Each pouch contained one grenade, the majority of which were shrapnel grenades that exploded upon contact with their tips. I also had illumination rounds (called “sunshine” or flares) to light up an area at night and greenies, which lit up like green firecrackers. Green was the signal for friendly forces and was used when we needed to tell others (e.g., helicopter gunships) of our position. The sunshine and greenies packed small parachutes that released at the peak of their altitude, enabling them to float slowly downward as the sunshine lit a night sky or the greenie notified friendlies of our status. The rounds were color coded and slid into the pouches with the tips aimed toward the ground so you could easily grab the backside and insert it into the weapon. The shrapnel grenades were designed with a safety feature—they would not explode until after they rotated two to five times once they were fired. For instance, if one hit a close tree branch when fired in a jungle, it would not explode and blow up the soldier who had fired it. The M79 grenade launcher reminded me of an old twelve-gauge shotgun that my dad had given me when I was twelve years old to use on my first hunt with him and some of his friends. They both were single-shot weapons that loaded by pushing a thumb lever, which allowed the gun to hinge open so the operator could insert the shell. The differences were that the M79 grenade launcher did not have much kick, and it had a distinctive “bloop” sound when fired.

I was excited about being the squad’s grenadier. I rearranged my vest and put the explosive grenades on top and down the middle. The sunshine grenades were placed on the left side and the greenies on my right. I wanted to be able to quickly find the correct grenade in the dark or when under fire.

My Colt .45-caliber pistol was meant as a backup weapon for close encounters. Like the M79, I had handled it one time in training, at which time I fired an entire magazine consisting of seven rounds plus the one round in the chamber. It was the first time in my life I had fired a handgun, and my accuracy was poor at best. I was fortunate that I would never have to use it in combat.

Our nights consisted of either an ambush patrol or guarding our platoon perimeter while the other squads went on patrol. Since each platoon had three rifle squads and one always stayed in on perimeter watch, we normally sent out two squads on ambush patrols. I had been in the bush approximately ten days (and in the country two weeks) when our nightly mission was to patrol and set up in an ambush site overlooking the Han River, near the same area where the two marines had drowned. It was common knowledge that the enemy used this waterway to move supplies at night. At around 0200, a member of our squad spotted movement near the middle of the river. Our radioman called in the sighting and got permission to fire blooper rounds at the target. The squad leader instructed me to blow up the raft, or whatever it was that we spotted.

The M79 is designed to launch special grenade rounds (shaped like super fat bullets) at an elevated angle. The grenadier aims the weapon at the proper loft to drop the round on or near its objective. It has pop-up sights for the grenadier to use in order to properly aim at his target. This requires him to first estimate the distance to the desired impact point and then to aim through an applicable marked distance point on the sight before squeezing the trigger. These pop-up sights were useless in the dark, where the grenadier had to rely on experience, a guess, and a prayer. I discovered later that most grenadiers never used the sights even in the daytime (some even removed them) but rather estimated the loft as related to the distance from past experience and feel.

I was now commanded to fire my M79 at an enemy raft at night. I excitedly, but blindly, pointed my grenade launcher a little higher than the target and fired. The river was approximately eighty feet wide at the point where we had set up our ambush. There was an explosion on the bank at the opposite side. Oops! It was nearly twice the distance. Someone in the squad yelled, “Shoot right at it!” I reloaded and fired again, this time directly at the center of the river without any loft. There was no explosion. My squad leader later said that the round skipped like a stone across the river. Without a loft, the round must have hit the water on its side and then skipped along until it finally sank or came to a stop on the opposite bank. On my third attempt, I aimed fairly high (nearly straight up) and successfully hit near the center of the river with an explosion that sounded like someone doing a cannonball in a swimming pool. I continued to fire until my squad leader yelled, “Hold your fire!” Of course, by this time the enemy had to be well down the waterway. Grenades exploding in water send a shock wave that has a paralyzing effect on any living being within a radius of twenty or more feet. This knowledge had come from our training in one of the infantry classes after boot camp. According to others in our squad, the enemy soldiers had disappeared into the water when they heard the first detonation on the opposite bank and were likely well past any danger from the later explosions. I was disappointed that I had let my unit down and that I had missed an opportunity to get my first confirmed kills. It would be my first and last chance to kill the enemy with my M79. The only other times I used it were to launch night sunshine (illumination rounds).

During our training, one instructor had said that grenadiers became so adept with the bloop gun that they could drop a round just about anywhere they desired. He claimed that marines were not satisfied with simply killing the enemy. They preferred to drop a round on their heads so they could watch their skulls explode and brains scatter. This had gotten a good laugh. It is doubtful that anyone could be that accurate with this weapon, and most of us realized it, even if we preferred to believe his story. This type of sick military humor had been part of our training, especially among some of the ego-strong instructors who had returned from Vietnam, some of who displayed multiple facial and body scars from bullet and shrapnel wounds. My scout-sniper instructor had told us not to shoot the kids because headquarters would not credit them as confirmed kills. I met half-dozen Vietnam veterans claiming to have shot an elephant while on patrol in the jungle, some of which boasted to have saved their entire unit by preventing the bull from leading its herd on a stampede towards them. Other marines had claimed they had necklaces of ears that they had detached from dead gooks with their Ka-Bar (knife). Whatever!

Notes: Although I do not have firsthand knowledge, Vietnam does have elephants, and there was a part of our tactical area of responsibility aptly named Elephant Valley (near Hill 180). Early in the war, the North Vietnamese Army used elephants to ship supplies south. This resulted in some of the elephants being killed, mostly by bombing raids on the Ho Chi Minh Trail. Taking out their four-legged transporters made good military sense.

There are no documented cases of Americans collecting ears (it would have resulted in a court-martial), but it was "tittle-tattle" widely spread by some returning veterans and picked up by the press.

There were many times when nothing exciting happened. When on night watch, I would occasionally glance upward. Vietnam had the most beautiful night sky I will ever know, especially on moonless nights. The prohibition of visible lights and campfires in the villages, the scarcity of clouds, and our placement in the middle of it all facilitated the sighting of more stars than I had ever seen. The setting provided a pitch-black backdrop for our galaxy's gleaming display. Although light-years away, the stars were comforting in this strange land and created a blanketed feeling of being closer to home.

We spent most of the daytime talking, preparing and eating C rations, and doing personal things such as writing home or reading books. It was difficult to sleep in the heat and humidity. Most of us had never heard of a country named Vietnam just a few years prior. We were a bunch of guys who happened to turn eighteen at a time in history when our country was at war. Our fatherland was calling, we answered, and they sent us to this small Indo-Chinese nation nine to ten thousand miles from our homes. It was a part of the baby boomer generation, as were assassinations of public figures, riots on college campuses, rock bands, and drugs. Soldiers who fight in a war rarely understand the politics surrounding their participation. This is probably meant to be. As my drill instructor would often say, “Yours is not to reason why, but to kill or die.” Regardless of that poetic guidance, we would from time to time give our “educated thoughts” on political aspects of the war. On one of those occasions, the subject of college riots was discussed. While attending Ohio State, two of my close high school buddies were attending Kent State University in Kent, Ohio. I occasionally visited them on weekends. Prior to my leaving for Vietnam, four demonstrators had been killed on the Kent campus by the Ohio National Guard. Being familiar with the area, I explained the campus layout to my new brothers in an effort to contribute to our conversation, but no one seemed to care much. Butch, who at twenty-one was one of the older and wiser guys in our squad summed it all up: “Shit happens.”

After Butch summed up the Kent State shootings with his profound words, we nodded or repeated them. “Yep, shit happens.” That was about as deep as we ever got on the subject of the war and our country’s purpose in being there. The politics back home and the angry public outcry did not seem to matter since it was too late for us to do anything about the Vietnam War—except fight in it.

Besides, there were more noteworthy items of discussion other than politics—like hot pants. We were aware that the newest trend back home was hot pants, and most girls our age were wearing them.

Personal hygiene was important. Although we were living in foxholes and humping most of our gear in rucksacks, we were still expected to shave daily (unless on a special mission, usually into the mountains), brush our teeth, and bathe and wash our clothes as often as we could find an available river. Everyone had a pair of shorts, or cutoff khakis, and most of us had extra pairs of socks. When we were camped during the day, most of us wore shorts and sandals but no shirt. While in the bush, we did not wear undershorts due to the high (sticky) humidity. This is now referred to as "going commando."

On occasion, we would smoke pot. During my college days, I had been introduced to marijuana. Students had to be living in a turtle shell not have been exposed to it. I was never much of a pothead, but I would take a whiff of a reefer when it was handed to me before passing it down the line. In our unit, pot smoking was done in the open during the day, and no one seemed to mind. I learned later that not all platoons were afforded this luxury because some had stricter company and platoon commanders, but at the time, I figured that every unit in Vietnam was free to smoke pot. When we went on a daytime combat mission—for example, to a heavily infested enemy territory or an area notorious for booby traps—the days were spent on patrols and high-alert perimeter watch. I did not witness any pot smoking during these times. In other words, most of the potheads were still trustworthy combatants.

One lazy and peaceful day, a few of us were playing with the local village children. It was hard to get used to the fact that we could be in a combat zone, miles from inhabited villages, worried about snipers and booby traps, and see a half dozen boys, ages eight to ten years old, appear with cold beer, Coca-Cola, and sometimes their older "virgin" sisters. As youngsters, they enjoyed our humor and teasing, but they were not allowed inside our compound. One of the guys in our squad, Ed Johnson (not his real name), decided to take them fishing at a nearby pond—marine style. I went along and watched him pull the pin of an M67 grenade and toss it into the water. It confirmed that an underwater explosion would stun and kill living beings. Four or five small fish came floating to the surface. I waded out in my shorts to get them for the kids, who were anxious to take them home to their families. When I came back to shore with the fish, others noticed that I had leeches on both legs. They looked like fat fishing worms just hanging on me, except they were dangling by their teeth—which were munched tightly into my skin—sucking my blood. There were at least a dozen of them. I quickly pulled the first one off and noticed a watery blood oozing out of my leg. That was when I remembered an instructor in the States warning us never to pull leeches off, but rather to burn their heads (after he told us not to wade into ponds). A couple of others in our platoon started touching them with cigarettes and they fell right off. The corpsman put some antiseptic on their bite marks, and they all healed within a few days.

During this time, we were ordered by our battalion commander not to buy anything from the illegal vendors—including beer, Coke, or any other goods from the kids. The black market in Vietnam was a serious problem. Some of the money spent by the GIs was channeled to the VC to buy food and supplies. To help prevent the funneling of real money to the black market, we were paid in military payment certificates (MPCs). It was illegal for us to have any other currency in our possession. We had been required to exchange all other foreign currencies (including American dollars) for MPCs once we entered the country. It was our “Monopoly money” and was used by all soldiers in Vietnam for the purpose of discouraging the black market. The MPCs looked a lot like money from a Monopoly™ game—about the same size with a different color for each denomination. The bills ranged from five cents to twenty dollars. We were paid monthly according to the amount we had earlier specified to be taken from our earnings. Once we left Vietnam, MPCs were worthless, but we could convert up to $600 for credit into our accounts. I normally asked for fifty to one hundred dollars per pay period to cover haircuts, extra cigarettes and toiletries from the BX, and beer and Coke from the kids. Some men who were gamblers had to find ways to launder their winnings if they totaled over $600 prior to going home, normally through buddies who didn’t keep a lot of cash.

Although our “Monopoly” money effectively slowed down their purchases, our enemy used a portion of it successfully. When we purchased from the kids, some of our money was likely going to support our opposition. It was my understanding that the military’s “approved vendors” were able to exchange their MPCs for the country’s currency (dong). Examples of approved vendors included the barbers who cut our hair, the servers who worked in the base saloon, and the maids who cleaned the officers’ quarters. These locals were all paid in MPC, and they later exchanged it for dong. Many of them received tips, especially the lady servers in the base saloon. In addition, vendors in the cities (Da Nang, Saigon, etc.) accepted MPCs and legally exchanged them for dong. Some of these vendors and storeowners laundered black market MPCs with the money that they received legally from the GIs. No one knows how much of this money was ultimately funneled to the VC, but I was told later by our company executive officer that it was fairly easy to do and was an ongoing problem.

It was disappointing not getting my daily cold Coca-Cola, but it was especially disheartening to the kids who brought it to us. Three or four days after the battalion commander prohibited us from buying cold drinks from the children, one of our squads tripped a booby trap. They were returning to our compound from a night ambush and were only approximately two hundred meters out. Two marines were medevaced with serious injuries. It was my first experience with this type of danger, although I was well aware of it due to stateside classes and warnings from many returning veterans. While I only knew the two injured marines in a casual way, I was exceedingly angry—once I got over the shock of what had happened. It did not seem right that someone would set a land mine with the intention of maiming or killing other human beings. Regardless of the innumerable times I had been warned about booby traps, my first reality of it was dumbfounding. I still get pissed thinking about them.

Our platoon sergeant, who was on his second tour in Vietnam, claimed the booby trap was set because we stopped dealing with the vendors. It made sense. They were not going to blow us up as long as we bought beer, Coke, and other goods from their children. If his reasoning was accurate, we were paying the enemy (through the kids) for our safety when we bought their goods. It reminded me of a time in high school when a few buddies and I went to a Cincinnati Reds baseball game at Crosley Field (approximately a hundred miles from our hometown). We had to street-park in a section of the inner city. A boy about eight to ten years old walked up to us and said he would "watch" our car for a dollar. There were four of us, and we each gave him a quarter. When we returned, our car was just as we had left it.

After the booby trap incident, our lieutenant allowed the vendors back (without informing the battalion commander), and things returned to normal—other than the unease we felt when leaving and returning to our compounds. The reason for the booby trap will never be explicitly determined. Planting booby traps was what gooks did.

1.4. The Accidental Loss of Lives

In war, there are teenagers and young men from all walks of life attempting to survive together as they travel and sleep with loaded guns, grenades, and other explosives (claymore mines, C-4 plastic explosives, hand pop flares). Proper safety habits, discipline, and cohesion are all necessary ingredients to help prevent accidents. A good combat squad must be consistently aware of gun- and explosives-safety practices, taught in stateside training. Unfortunately, many soldiers learn safety habits the hard way—from accidents that take lives or severely injure others; or by near misses, such as when a weapon accidentally discharges but does not hurt anyone. On-the-job lessons in civilian terms are sometimes branded as the "school of hard knocks," but in war they could be termed "teachings from the wounded and dead."

During my initial tour in the bush, I learned of a firefight my squad had against each other prior to my joining them. This type of event was all too common and simply acknowledged as a friendly firefight. The average strength of most squads in Vietnam was between ten and thirteen men. Ideally, a marine rifle squad consisted of three teams of four men each, plus the squad leader, but we were not always at full strength. The squad leader carried a topographic map of the marine tactical area of responsibility, on which he would mark the coordinates given to him for his squad's nightly ambush site, including checkpoint coordinates. As the leader, he was responsible for determining the exact spot to set up the ambush as well as designing its structure. The structure was normally dictated by the terrain and its natural barriers (rivers, cliffs, rocks), but it could also be determined by other factors, including the amount of moonlight, the expanse of dry area (especially in rice paddies), the squad leader's preferences, and how many guys were going to stay awake at one time (usually determined by his danger assessment). Some squad leaders placed everyone close together and kept only one man awake. This enabled everyone to get more sleep as each marine would pass his watch to someone else after as little as forty-five minutes. Marine policy required that everyone stay awake on all ambushes, and our general policy in Vietnam was a minimum of 50 percent had to be awake. However, this was a war where rules were broken, and this was sometimes a place without rules. Moonless nights were normally the most dangerous. The villagers in the countryside were not allowed outside lights at night, creating a completely dark ambiance. When there was no moonlight, it was hard to see your hand when held just inches from your face. The thousands of twinkling stars could not equal the light of even the last few phases of a waning moon. These dark nights belonged to the VC. On moonless or nearly pitch-dark nights, the indigenous enemy enjoyed a tremendous advantage, as it could quietly move throughout its familiar homeland undetected. They were like shadows in the night, moving into deadly ambush positions, setting booby traps, and resupplying their troops with ammunition, supplies, and personnel.

On the night that the two members of the squad had fired upon each other, the squad leader had set up in an L-shaped pattern, with the marines facing the inside of the angle, starting at the intersection where two paths crossed. Each leg of the L stretched laterally in both directions with six marines on one leg and five on the other. They had been tightly formed, with one marine from each leg on watch as the others took turns sleeping. Squads in Vietnam consisted of both soldiers who had been in country for a while (salts) and soldiers recently out of boot camp (boots), also known as FNGs (fuckin' new guys). This was different from past wars, where entire units were deployed together. The combination of salts and boots could prove dangerous, and this had been one of those occasions. L-shaped ambush settings were supposed to be open or obtuse in nature. On this night, they had been set up to guard the union of both paths, forcing the squad into a ninety-degree setting, if not an even tighter acute angle. This type of set was acceptable if the soldiers were facing out. For example, we were taught even tighter V-shaped setups with everyone facing back-to-back.

Late into the night, a salty marine with only two weeks left in country had stood up to relieve himself when a boot facing him on the opposite end of the L awoke, panicked, and opened fire. It was not unusual for salts to take such liberties when they knew the squad was set up in a relatively safe location. However, the newly in-country marine thought it was a VC coming down the path and was too inexperienced and jittery to rationalize otherwise. Jittery marines were referred to as "squirrely" by the salts. The setup, with the marines facing inward, enabled the salt and the squirrely boot—on opposite ends of the L—to engage in a firefight with each other. Both marines died in the exchange.

After listening to these events, my attitude changed from a gung-ho marine willing to obliterate the enemy to a more rational one of "You had better wise up quickly around here, Dave." Four marines in my squad alone died just prior to my joining it—the two who had tried to swim after dead bodies and the two who had inadvertently shot each other. It was not going to be as simple as I had naïvely imagined, with thoughts similar to shooting slow-moving ducks at a carnival-gallery game. I was meeting the reality of nonfiction war and obtaining essential knowledge that would prove invaluable once I was promoted to squad leader later in my tour. I learned over time that the inadvertent loss of our own was largely due to the lack of leadership or knowledge, stupidity, carelessness, or the combination of two or more of these human weaknesses.

Historical note: There were 58,220 American deaths in Vietnam reported as of April 29, 2008. Non-hostile deaths were 10,663 (18.3 percent), and hostile deaths were 47,434. The majority of the non-hostile deaths were by accidents (9,107). The remaining were illness (938), homicide (236), and classified as self-inflicted (382).[4]

During my time as a boot, I was the opposite of squirrely and probably too cautious. During my third week in Vietnam, we were on a night ambush in a rice paddy, set up in a tight, curve-type formation and facing out towards a foot-high dyke. I had recently come off my watch and was sleeping soundly when I was awakened by gunfire. The marine next to me, who was now on watch, had opened fire on an enemy squad moving through our ambush site only thirty to forty meters from us. The enemy immediately returned fire. I awoke not realizing what was happening, or where I was, and experienced a strange, overwhelming feeling. I just wanted to stand up and yell for both sides to stop trying to kill each other and talk this over. However, I reacted as trained and pointed my M79 toward the enemy as I experienced for the first time the zing of bullets whistling past me. Realizing we were too close for a grenade launcher, I reached for my .45-caliber pistol. In a matter of seconds, the firefight was over, and the squad leader yelled out for each team leader to give him a casualty report. Everyone was okay. The squad leader instructed me to fire sunshine. I removed the explosion grenade from my M79, replaced it with an illumination round, aimed straight up, and fired. Fortunately, I did not fire it exactly straight above us, and the round exploded over the enemy's position. I loaded and fired another one, now remembering not to fire sunshine over our position or between the enemy and us. The proper placement should be just behind them, where their silhouettes could be distinguished but not ours. I continued to fire illumination rounds, each one just prior to the previous one burning out or floating to the ground.

We soon heard the loud sounds of mortars being launched from our firebase. The squad leader had called for longer lasting mortar illumination rounds. They exploded overhead, and the night sky around us was turned into day. It was not necessary for me to launch any more of my rounds. The squad leader sent a team to inspect the area. They found blood but no bodies. Afterward, we were instructed to end our ambush early, and we returned to our platoon's perimeter. This was common procedure after an engagement with the enemy, since our position and presence in the area were compromised (also referred to as "time to get out of Dodge").

I later felt guilty that I (the gung-ho marine) had not even fired a single shot and that I experienced a wimpy feeling of wanting to mediate instead of kill. I kept the latter to myself, but it showed how true feelings can override temporary brainwashing when tested in a real situation. It was a reaction that I would never feel again as I realized that the enemy was trying to kill me. My perspective toward war morphed into an offensive, battle-tested assertiveness—a necessity of survival for soldiers in warfare. I also noticed that I was able to awaken (for any reason) with a comprehensive sense of my surroundings.

Later in my tour, a most horrible accident occurred. There was danger in being too gung-ho—and therefore too trigger-happy. A Cobra helicopter, seemingly patrolling on its own, spotted what its pilot surmised as enemy troop movement, but was our third platoon moving its position. Without verification or permission to fire, the Cobra came in with its guns blaring. The marines were in open terrain with nowhere to take cover. The chopper's initial attack ended quickly, and it banked to its right to come in for a second attack. One of the squad leaders launched a green flare, causing the pilot to pull up just prior to his second assault. Our field radios were typically not on the pilot's frequency, but our platoon radioman was able to move to it and assure the chopper that we were friendlies. He next moved to the medevac frequency.

The platoon had taken some serious casualties. Two of them were close friends, Trojan (not his real nickname) and Alabama (his real nickname). Both men had spent time in the rear when I was the company's awards writer and had requested to return to the bush around the same time as me. Alabama had become one of my best friends in Vietnam. He had a quiet, easygoing personality and could find humor in just about anything. Tragically, Alabama died from wounds caused by friendly fire.

Trojan was one of the platoon's grenadiers. Bullets hit some of the rounds on his ammo vest, detonating them. He lived, but the explosions resulted in the amputation of his left leg and his left arm, and he lost an eye. Trojan was also our platoon's guitar player and instructor while we were all in the rear. I would sit with him on occasion, and he would teach me a few chords on his guitar. After the accident, I bought a guitar from a Vietnamese store in Da Nang and continued practicing what he had taught me.

This was the most senseless act of all friendly accidents during my tour. I had heard of similar incidents when I was stateside; therefore, I knew it was not uncommon.

One week after the helicopter shootings, another friend lost his life when he stood up while in an ambush setting to relieve himself and was shot by a boot. Kali (not his real name) from Hawaii was in Fox Company's third platoon and had recently celebrated his twentieth birthday. Kali was a smart marine and had to have felt safe or he would not have stood up while at an ambush sight. This type of loss was also too common of an occurrence.

Vietnam was too often a rogue, discipline-deficient war—at the expense of safety and lives.

1.5. Gooks

We were fighting two primary enemies:

The VC was the local Communist force in South Vietnam and the primary enemy in our tactical area of responsibility. We commonly referred to them as Victor Charlie, or just Charlie. This came from the military phonetic alphabet of Victor for the letter *V* and Charlie for the letter *C*. The phonetic alphabet was used for radio communications to assure clarity. When we were communicating via the radio, a VC killed in action would be reported as "Victor Charlie, Kilo India Alpha"; wounded in action would be "Whiskey India Alpha." One of my favorite inside jokes came years later, from the movie *Forrest Gump,* when Forrest (played by Tom Hanks) said, "We was always taking long walks, and we was always looking for a guy named Charlie."[5]

The VC could have been any one of the natives. This included some of the "friendly" Popular Forces who sometimes camped with us, and the local people living in the villages and cities, including women and children. They were Communist fighters and sympathizers, in contrast to the local friendly forces that were on our side. The good guys included the Army of the Republic of Vietnam (ARVN), the Popular Forces (PFs), the Regional Forces (RFs), and the supportive civilians. The safest way to distinguish the friendly forces from the VC combatants was by their clothing. The friendlies wore uniforms and the VC wore black pajama-type outfits at night, but they dressed like civilians during the day. I'm not sure that most the people in the South understood democracy or desired it, but they did support their independence from the North. I also believe that many of them took the side of whoever they thought would be the ultimate winner. This was conceivably learned from the First Indochina War, between the French-backed South Vietnamese forces and the Communists (identified during that time as the local Vietminh and the northern Communists). When the French left, the local French sympathizers suffered the consequences of the victor's wrath. The French displayed no lasting loyalty to their Vietnam comrades and left them to be slaughtered, raped, imprisoned, and abused in unimaginable ways. Therefore, some locals played both sides as a way to hedge their later survival. It was possible for a South Vietnamese native to be a Communist VC while serving in the local Popular Forces, supposedly fighting for democracy. These locals were not fighting for democracy or communism but for self-preservation.

The VC's military fortes were booby traps, small hit-and-vanish night ambushes, solitary day and nighttime sniper assaults, rocket attacks, and grenadier attacks. In our tactical area of responsibility, we battled the legendary Phantom Blooper, a VC grenadier who would shoot a couple of grenades at a platoon of marines during the night and then vanish.

Note: Estimates of South Vietnamese citizens who died from political violence at the hands of Communist forces after US withdrawal in 1975 range from four-hundred thousand to 2.5 million.[6] There are no records on the number of citizens imprisoned or tortured.

Another prominent enemy was the North Vietnamese Army (NVA). These were the North's combat-ready soldiers, aptly trained in regimental-style boot and infantry camps. The NVA moved down the Ho Chi Minh Trail from North Vietnam daily. US forces would sometimes "visit" them via secret and illicit missions into the jungles and mountains in the neighboring countries of Laos or Cambodia, where the NVA maintained base camps to stage soldiers, big guns, weapons, and supplies.

We commonly referred to all enemy forces as "gooks," a term originally used for our enemy in the Korean War. It was a derogatory term referring only to enemy forces. We were young men thrust into a war theater and given hunting licenses, rifles, and unlimited amount of ammunition. It was a way to dehumanize our targets. Gooks (not human beings) were our game, and there were no bag limits. Although some may have initially viewed it as a sport, we all knew that anyone we shot had better be an enemy combatant. Later, I heard that the politically-correct, non-military citizens back home claimed this to be a racial slur. I guess I should apologize to all the kind-hearted men and women who were trying to kill me or blow my limbs off for calling them gooks. I am so sorry.

The VC, our primary nemesis during my tour of duty in Vietnam, rarely engaged in direct confrontations but they were nonetheless a formidable foe. The VC constructed miles of secret tunnels and used these to move beneath us without our detection. These underground channels led to secret hotels, armories, and hospitals. They used this extensive tunnel system to move into tactical locations and launch night ambushes before vanishing as mere glimmers in the night. During the years of US military involvement, we were not aware of the enormity of their underground subways. We were prepared to fight a traditional war where we sought out the enemy and pelted it with rapid small arms fire along with artillery and air support. Even though American soldiers knew of the tunnels and found many of them, it was years after the war that the United States became aware of the extensiveness of this system. This is dumbfounding because the enemy not only used its tunnel-disappearing act thousands of times on US troops from 1965 to 1973, but it used the same tactic while defeating the French in a war that lasted from 1946 to 1954.

Notes: Popular Vietnam contemporary tourist sites include the tunnels of Cu Chi, in and around the South Vietnamese capital of Ho Chi Minh City (Saigon until 1976). There are reportedly 155 miles of tunnels in this area alone that were originally started as protection against French air raids.[7]

It was also learned later that the VC had tunnels beginning underwater on the banks of the rivers and rising upward above water level, allowing them to bring weapons and supplies down the rivers and into their underground networks without moving across land.

A good example of how the VC outfoxed us using their tunnel system is exemplified by, "cordon-and-search" operations that we regularly carried out. Intelligence had evidence that certain villages sympathized with the VC (known to us as a VC village). This included housing, feeding, and doctoring VC troops. A cordon-and-search mission consisted of quietly moving in and surrounding a VC village just before daylight thus trapping everyone in the village and forcing anyone trying to escape to have to break our perimeter. We knew that the VC normally ended their patrols well before daylight and would therefore be back in their respective villages before we slipped in and surrounded them. Once daylight hit, special agents, officers, senior enlisted men, and local interpreters would go into the village and search for VC. They would comb inside each dwelling, looking for Vietnamese without the proper papers (the South Vietnamese government and the United States required all Vietnamese people to carry identification). I took part in two cordon-and-search operations and was told that neither one resulted in even one captured VC; although on one raid we "captured" two local women who did not have papers.

Fast-forward to a sleepless night years after I left Vietnam: It occurred to me how we could have won the war against the VC, thus eliminating this key central element from the northern Communists. The failure of our cordon-and-search operations never made a lot of sense because we were sure that there was VC in the villages that we secretly surrounded at night and searched the next morning. What if we had identified the tunnel system and used their own sanctuaries to trap them? I now believe we could have found many of the VC with a bulldozer/backhoe combination (with tank tracks) that is commonly used in construction all over the world. The machines could have been brought to the VC villages via Sikorsky CH-54 helicopters. After conducting our cordon-and-search of each suspected VC village, we could have simply dug a trench around each village with the backhoe, uncovering the tunnels. As we pursued the underground channels with the backhoe, we would likely have unearthed the VC, their weapons, ammunition, wounded, and documents. Afterward, we could have restored the land with the bulldozer part of the backhoe/bulldozer.

As I look back, digging them up makes sense. The way we were operating was similar to looking for bad guys on the first floor of one-story buildings and not realizing they were in the basements sleeping and eating breakfast.

Note: The Sikorsky CH-54 Skycrane was a helicopter used in Vietnam for transporting tanks or picking up downed helicopters and returning them to a base for repair.[8] These heavy-duty transporters could have also carried bulldozers.

1.6. Communications

Our platoon of approximately fifty men normally traveled and camped together during the daytime. The platoon radioman carried a field radio (PRC-25), and each of the three combat squads carried one also. The field radios were our main means of communication, especially when separated (usually at night on ambush patrols). Humping a radio was one of the toughest jobs in Vietnam. In addition to the extra weight (the PRC-25 weighed approximately twenty-five pounds), the radioman carried the additional stress of responsibility. On many occasions, our radio was the only link between isolation and support. It was used by each squad to report its position back to its platoon, make medevac requests, direct tactical air requests (call for fire), give pilot briefings—both chopper and fighter planes—and make simple everyday ration and supply orders. Each of these call stations had a different frequency band, obtained by adjusting two knobs on the PRC-25. The radioman had to have the knowledge to accurately set the right frequency and keep valiant composure while communicating under fire.

The radioman was in more danger than most other soldiers. The enemy knew the value of taking out a squad's radio and radioman, thus preventing him from calling for fire support or reinforcements. As a sniper, I was trained to first determine and remove the squad leader, followed by the radioman. Our instructor said that a sniper had the capability of firing a round through the radio and into the back of the radioman, eliminating them both.

We used two primary types of green signals to rapidly communicate that we were friendlies: "greenie" rounds fired by M79 grenade launchers and green pop flares carried by members of each squad. I carried green pop flares along with illumination pop flares. These were small, skinny tubes similar to maritime-distress flares. It was necessary to set off a green flare every time we returned from a night ambush to let the marines guarding our perimeter know that friendlies were returning. I would simply take a flare, remove the lid (with the firing pin enclosed), place it on the bottom of the flare, and aim it where I wanted it to go (somewhere not over our position or the platoon's position). While holding it with my left hand, I would hit it with the palm of my right hand, causing it to shoot up and explode like a small rocket. Green signals were a preliminary notification of friendly forces to prevent an immediate assault. The enemy knew this color signal, so we always verified these first alerts by radio when we were unsure of the people or units initiating them.

At times, it was necessary to communicate with the natives. The locals did not understand English very well, and we knew very little Vietnamese. We quickly learned that sternly stating, "*Dung lai*" meant, "Don't move" and that screaming "*Lai dai*" meant, "Come here." Telling someone to "*Didi mau*" (or "*Didi*") was "Go away."

There was a mingled terminology that both sides understood and used often:

Boo-coo meant "a lot" or "very much" and was a favorite word of US soldiers and the Vietnamese people. For example, they might tell us: "Coke boo-coo cold" or "Sister boo-coo virgin." We might answer, "You boo-coo lie."

Same-same meant "alike," or one of whatever was the same as another of whatever. It was surprising how much this word was used. For example, if someone bought a beer and you wanted one too, you would say, "Same-same."

Party pack was ten rolled marijuana cigarettes in a package.

Number one simply meant "best." The Vietnamese might say, "Party pack boo-coo number one."

Number ten meant, "worst." We might say to a local whom we suspected of being the enemy, "*Dung lai*" and then point at the person and say, "Boo-coo number-ten VC."

We were all so bilingual!

We were also taught about a program using the words "*chieu hoi*," a term that the enemy recognized as "surrender." The United States distributed pamphlets throughout South Vietnam with instructions on how the enemy could lay down its weapons and turn itself over to our side. We were given additional instructions on how and how not to treat prisoners. For example, we were to isolate them, but we were not allowed to mistreat them or to refuse them water or medical attention. Prisoners who surrendered were taken to a *chieu hoi* camp and transformed into friendly fighters if possible. Some became Kit Carson scouts, who went along on designated missions with us. This was a good program.

Notes: Kit Carson scouts were enemy combatants who surrendered and were transformed into scouts assigned to Marine Corps platoons. They were good interpreters and point men, and they recognized many of the enemy's tactics, preventing marine casualties.[9]

After the northern Communists successfully invaded the South (1975), Kit Carson scouts were classified as traitors and executed.

1.7. Choppers

Prior to entering the Marine Corps, I had a friend who was instantly killed when a rotating blade from a helicopter hit him while he was either boarding or departing. Therefore, I was always very cautious when I was doing the same. I probably ducked lower than others did. It became obvious how chopper blades could cause horrifying accidents. In Vietnam, the chopper pilots often landed on uneven ground or hovered a few feet above the ground while we jumped out. Ideally, both bottom runners should land horizontally on level ground, touching at relatively the same time. If one side of the chopper is angled, the blades are closer to the ground on the lower side. This was often the case on takeoff from uneven terrain, when the chopper might angle sideways, and its mighty blades would swing dangerously nearer to the ground. However, the pilots were skilled at keeping the blades amply above the ground in the areas where we embarked and disembarked. When finding a landing zone for a chopper, we always looked for the most level ground possible that was farthest from enemy fire. Sometimes, neither one of these was possible. The chopper pilots would try to rescue wounded soldiers in almost any situation, including bad weather, bad terrain, and in hot (enemy fire) landing zones. The pilots and machine gunners on a chopper were said to have the shortest average life spans of all soldiers in Vietnam.

Note: A total of 2,165 helicopter pilots were killed in the Vietnam War, along with 2,712 crewmembers. These figures do not include troops killed in transit.[10]

In Vietnam, a grunt "enjoyed" a lot of chopper rides. Helicopters seemed to be everywhere, and we joked that the helicopter was the official bird of Vietnam. Jumping on and off a chopper never became routine as I always felt added adrenaline and an enormous pride at being a warrior important enough to be chauffeured by air to our next assignment. We sat shoulder to shoulder in the back of a CH-46 (sometimes referred to as a Phrog) or the larger C-53. There were two ways to get around—hump or take a chopper. If we were going two to three miles, we would usually hump. Longer distances were in a big bird. Either way could be dangerous. Humping meant the high probability of booby traps or enemy fire. Choppers always risked the possibility of a crash due to enemy fire, weather conditions, rough terrain, or mechanical failure. Many missions incorporated the best of both—chopper to an open or safe site and then hump to our final coordinates.

Selected missions incorporated dozens of choppers, each loaded with marines and corpsmen and flying so near to each other that I could see the gunners' faces in the choppers on each flank. It was quite a sight, and I felt proud to be part of such substantial military undertakings. If the landing zone were large enough, the choppers would land relatively close to the same time. On many occasions, we would start to jump out as soon as we were within five or six feet of the ground, and quickly organize a perimeter with everyone facing outward toward an anticipated enemy. Leaving a mission was often quite dangerous and the most likely time to take enemy fire. On one occasion, the machine gunner on our starboard side began firing, as we were still loading and about to take off in a CH-46 after a short mission just north of Charlie

Ridge. The pilot began his ascent while the last marines were hurrying up the back ramp as it was closing. The last two marines, including the squad leader, turned and began to fire blindly out the back. I had no idea what I was supposed to do, or if I was allowed to fire my M79 grenade launcher from a chopper. I had not even heard the enemy's gunfire, probably due to the noise coming from the machine gunner's .60-caliber and the chopper blades. I was too new to distinguish and filter the individual sounds of this war. We quickly climbed out of danger, but being in a chopper while engaging in a firefight with the enemy created a feeling of near helplessness and required the need to trust others for my protection. Later, Butch and some of the other guys in my squad assured me that I should not fire a grenade launcher from a chopper for fear of hitting the blades if the chopper should bank the wrong way. I had been impressed by the chopper's machine gunner who initiated the firefight. He had been observing a specific area that he had assessed as a potential danger zone. I was also impressed by the instinctive reaction and return fire by members of my squad and felt that I would be ready to join in the fight if the opportunity presented itself again.

Choppers were favorite targets of enemy snipers, as attested by the number of them lost during the Vietnam War. There were 5,607 lost out of 11,835 deployed.[11] The enemy had knowledge of where to do so with rockets and AK-47 small-arms fire. To a competent sniper, it was a huge, slow blimp. It had to be a real boasting right for a gook to shoot down a large green bird loaded with enemy soldiers. Many times, helicopters exploded on impact with the ground. I witnessed this on one occasion when a chopper came in helplessly spinning in circles approximately one mile from our camp and crashed into the ground in a huge ball of flames, killing everyone on board.

After only forty-five days in the bush, I received word that I was being transferred to the rear to become the company's awards writer. I had two qualifications for this job: I had two quarters of English composition in college, and I had typed a whopping thirteen words per minute in a marine entry-exam typing test. I tried to refuse the assignment, but my lieutenant ordered me to "pack up and get your ass on the next chopper." At least for now, my chopper-riding and gook-hunting days were over.

Later that night, a marine in one of the other squads in our platoon was shot in the leg by a VC sniper while he was on perimeter watch. It was not serious, and he was treated by the corpsman and medevaced early the next morning. I traveled to the rear with him (per the lieutenant's orders—it was "the next chopper"). Once we landed, I helped him into a jeep, where he was to be taken to the Da Nang hospital. While waiting to be transported, he told me that he had made the mistake of lighting a cigarette. The sniper had obviously seen the light and fired at it, grazing his leg. He was lucky to be alive, and he knew it.

Part II

★★★

2.1. The Rear/Awards Writer

One of my first duties as the Fox Company's awards writer was to start on a backlog of honors for marines killed in action and to write follow-up letters to the parents or spouses detailing the cause of their loved one's death. This included the two marines who had drowned in the river while trying to recover the bodies of dead (VC). Fellow marines who witnessed this tragedy told me all about it when I first got to the bush. After all, I had been one of their replacements.

I began my work by researching past awards written by my predecessors. They all began and ended the same. The beginning: "For valor [courage, meritorious service] while serving with Company F, Second Battalion, First Marines in connection with combat operations against the enemy in the Republic of Vietnam, Private First Class Robert Smith, exposing himself to great personal risk…." There were two or three paragraphs in the middle describing the circumstances for the medal or the reason for the marine's death stressing heroism and including a description of the battle or circumstance for the correspondence or award. The ending: "Private First Class Robert Smith is a credit to his God, Family, and the United States Marine Corps."

Although I searched the files, I could not find examples of follow-up letters to loved ones or replies to inquiries from family members. I instinctively understood not to tell parents that their sons had died unnecessarily because a company commander wanted enemy bodies as proof of confirmed kills. Due to our initial notifications, the parents knew that their respective sons had drowned, which created something of a dilemma. After the initial salutation, I began the first letter: "While crossing the Han River, Joe's unit came under intense enemy fire." I then explained that, although he and the other marines immediately returned fire, Joe was overcome by the swift current and was swept downstream, where he was rescued and taken by helicopter to the Da Nang hospital. “Unfortunately, Joe was not able to be revived by the medical doctors.” I ended by expressing our deep regrets, and how well-liked he was by his unit (which was what many of the men had told me).

Yes, some of it was bullshit, but I was not ashamed to write it at that time, nor am I ashamed that I did it as of today. These two marines courageously died in the line of duty, and their loved ones should always be proud of them. Families suffered regardless of how their loved ones lost their lives.

The letter to the second family was similar to the first. Correspondence to families had to be signed by the company commander. However, he had given our first sergeant permission to sign his name on such matters. In this case, it was probably good that the first sergeant forged the signature on my letters, since the company commander was the same one who had ordered his men to “get those bodies.” In our commander’s defense, he was on his first tour of Vietnam and underestimated the danger of the swift current when he gave the order.

Later in my tour, two drug-related deaths happened in one night. One marine overdosed on heroin and asphyxiated on his vomit. The other was high on marijuana and dived off a tower while on guard duty, breaking his neck. I composed and typed the correspondence to their loved ones, but did not mention that drugs were involved. The company commander signed them, and I put them in the mailbag.

Our company headquarters accommodated the company's executive officer, first sergeant (E-8), office manager, radio coordinator, file clerk, two other miscellaneous office clerks, and me. Our first sergeant was known as Top (I have forgotten his actual name; he was always just Top). He was a salty marine who had been in the corps for over twenty-five years and was like an old bulldog with a loud bark but no bite. Top was a true hero—having been wounded in the Korean conflict—and loved to tell stories about how the marines fought and won battles under terrible conditions. Whenever we received a request from soldiers in the bush for new combat boots or some other need, he would spout out, "Hell, we didn't have new boots in the frozen Chosin." He would then make sure that new combat boots were shipped on the next chopper.

Historical note: The frozen Chosin (the Chosin Reservoir) was the site of a sequence of battles in the Korean War that took place in November 1950. Marines from the First Marine Division were outnumbered eight to one by Chinese forces and cut off from support as they survived the coldest winter North Korea had experienced in a hundred years. The marines fought their way through ten Chinese infantry units and embarked on a seventy-eight-mile journey to rejoin American forces.[12]

Everyone loved Top. I met the first sergeant on my second day of deployment in Vietnam. I was standing in formation with other new arrivals when I first heard his raspy voice: "Where the hell is Private Gerhardt?"

I had gotten accustomed to being shouted at by lifers in the States and just figured it was going to be the same in Vietnam. However, I was not going to be intimidated. "Here, First Sergeant," I loudly replied.

“Why the hell are you still a private?” he roared while walking toward me.

“I have no reason,” I quickly replied, remaining emotionless. He had hit on a sore topic. I felt that I had been overlooked in my previous assignments and had deserved a promotion over some of the others who had received them.

He looked me over and then said, “No 0311 with a good record is going to be paid private wages in my company.” He walked back into the company headquarters. A couple of days later, I was promoted to private first class (E-2). When I became an awards writer and I moved into the same company headquarters as Top, I learned that he had reviewed our files when we first arrived and had singled me as someone who should have been promoted at least once.

Note: 0311 is the Marine Corps classification for an infantry rifleman. Top was very protective of infantry soldiers, most likely because he was one himself.

Top was an excellent leader, commanding respect without demanding it. He gave me only one directive: “Get your hair cut every two weeks.” He added, “No fuckin’ longhairs are allowed in my house.” Lifers hated gooks, but they hated hippies more. I had already experienced this. During my time at Camp Pendleton, California, I was put in charge of a three-man (all of us privates) weekend patrol into the mountains. Camp Pendleton bordered San Clemente, the home of President Nixon when he was not in Washington, DC. The president was scheduled to stay in San Clemente that weekend. My staff sergeant said that a squad of longhairs had been spotted in the mountains, and that we were to guard against their infiltration of our base. I knew at the time—from common sense and the way he said it—that this was bullshit. The three of us were upset because it took away our weekend leave. The staff sergeant gave us a radio and said to check in with the base radio station "every few hours or so." I sarcastically asked him whether this was a combat or recon patrol. We were taught in one of our early classes that there were two types of patrols, combat and reconnaissance, with the difference being either to engage or destroy the enemy and his will to fight or to merely observe. He told me to "capture one of those assholes and drag him back here by his hair." After that, he left on weekend leave.

Lifers often talked about longhairs. Hippies embodied our opposites—in appearance and thought. At the time, Ronald Reagan was the governor of California. Our staff sergeant had one of Governor Reagan's quotes on his bulletin board: "A hippie looks like Tarzan, talks like Jane, and smells like Cheetah."

On Friday night, we humped to one of the highest peaks and camped there for two nights. We brought our M14 rifles (no ammo) and plenty of C rations, water, and cigarettes. A pack of coyotes stayed around us the entire time, keeping us awake at night with unremitting howling. They were skinny, straggly-looking creatures. We stayed on "lookout" until early Sunday morning and then humped down the mountain and back to our base. Prior to leaving, we opened our remaining C rations and left them for our hungry new friends.

2.2. Hang On, Sloopy

One day I received an unusual request from some of my comrades, suggesting that I write a posthumous award for a dog that had recently tripped a booby trap. Booby traps were a dangerous reality for all soldiers in Vietnam. A single explosion could kill and maim multiple warriors. The soldier who tripped one would often lose one or both of his legs and sometimes his arm or arms. The soldiers near him would receive shrapnel in their chests or heads, and they would often die from these wounds. Booby traps in our area mostly consisted of American, Russian, and Chinese explosives or improvised explosives (usually an American C ration or beer can loaded with C-4 and shrapnel). The VC also set “toe poppers,” consisting of a single bullet placed underground that would fire when stepped on. In the jungle, the enemy devised “punji sticks” placed in concealed pits or made to drop down out of trees and puncture the bodies of their victims with multiple wounds.

The US military trained dogs (called “war dogs”) to sniff out booby traps and to lead troops through mined areas as sacrificial nonhuman scouts. Mostly German Shepherds, these dogs exhibited a natural dedication to their troops along with unselfish bravery. They were smart and learned the danger posed by booby traps, but they were willing to sacrifice their lives for us. We became attached to our war dogs as they loved and served us.

Sloopy was a medium-sized female German Shepherd that seemed to want all American soldiers to like her. She knew the difference between the Americans and locals and was said to growl at Vietnamese civilians and soldiers who tried to get close to the marine perimeters. As a dog lover, I became attached to her and loved seeing her when she would come into the rear while I was an awards writer. We nicknamed her Sloopy after a popular song, “Hang on Sloopy,” that someone was playing on a tape recorder in our barracks one evening. Sloopy and her guide often came into our company headquarters, where I kept treats for her from the mess hall. She would sometimes lie at my feet as I typed. I think she enjoyed the soothing noise of the typewriter as well as the breeze from a fan we had in the office. She was well known in Fox Company for the time she sniffed out and pointed at a booby trap, thus saving marine lives. This time, Sloopy tripped a booby trap believed to be made of a Russian grenade and died shortly thereafter in her guide's arms. Her last brave act saved some of the marines she had loved and served so well. Everyone believed that our innocent, faithful friend deserved a posthumous award. And so it was.

Note: Sloopy's Bronze Star was unofficial at best. In 1943 during World War II, the army awarded Chips, a German Shepherd, the Silver Star and a Purple Heart for heroism under fire. The award was protested, and Congress got involved. After a three-month debate, it was decided that non-humans could not receive awards intended for humans. In order to ensure this, the military classified war dogs as equipment. The classification later enabled the military to leave this type of "equipment" behind after the Vietnam War.[13]

At the beginning of my new assignment, I was able to write posthumous letters and awards without a lot of heartfelt feeling. Once Sloopy was killed, because she had so captured my heart, I became affected by the words I was writing in a personal way. Until Sloopy's death, it had just been my job, and I had done my best to keep feelings out of it. As I wrote her award, I began to realize how sad it was to lose a life, especially a human life. This realization came from the guilty feeling I had from mourning a dog more than some of the marines who had sacrificed their lives. I had a natural block against these feelings—a wall that Sloopy knocked down with her death. I started to really hate gooks, and it was now personal.

Historical note: There were approximately 4,900 dogs used in Vietnam between 1964 and 1975, of which 204 returned home. Records of dogs and their fates were not kept. Therefore, no one knows how many were killed in action. Many dogs were left behind or euthanized.[14]

2.3. A Mother's Letter of Anguish

One afternoon, the executive officer handed me a handwritten letter he wanted me to answer, type, and make available for the company commander to read and sign the next day. Some of the words in the letter have had a haunting personal effect on me from the moment I read them to the present. It was from the heart-struck mother of a marine, Jake Brown (not his real name), who had died in action after serving less than two weeks in country. As I read her three handwritten pages, I could sense her anguish in the tear-stained pages. She wanted to know more about how her beloved son had died. Had he suffered? Had he said anything? Had any of his friends been with him, and could she write to them?

Her hurt turned into anger in the middle part of her letter as she lashed out at the agency she felt was responsible for his death. "Why did the Marine Corps take my nineteen-year-old son and send him off to war after only two months of boot camp and just sixty additional days of training? No nineteen-year-old is ready for war with such lack of readiness!" I do not remember what else she wrote.

I allowed her words to echo in my thoughts that night before formulating a reply. I recalled being handed a grenade launcher by my squad leader my second day in the bush, after only shooting one round from this weapon during training. I remembered the first time in combat when I shot a round towards the middle of the river and hit the bank on the other side—missing my target by approximately fifty feet. I was lucky that no friendlies were there. We had spent a week on the rifle range in boot camp, and each of us had to qualify in order to move on. There was similar training for the M79 grenade launcher and other weapons, but due to shortages, most infantrymen were rushed to join a combat unit without specialized-weapons training. During the Vietnam era, boot camp alone was two weeks shorter than in future times as we were rapidly moved through training and hurried to Vietnam. Since there were few tests and classes were not repeated, we either got it or didn't, and no one knew either way. I was fortunate to have spent extra time in the States, allowing some of my lessons to soak in while I grew a little wiser at this crucial age. I also had additional knowledge from well-taught lessons in scout sniper training. Soldiers who move from military training straight to combat do not have ample time to translate teachings into knowledge in a dangerously new and very unfamiliar profession. I have no idea if additional training would have saved Jake Brown. His mother was correct in that we had hurried her son into combat without being fully trained and tested. Of course, I could not reply with those thoughts, and I was at a loss for words.

I attempted to discuss the letter with my executive officer the following morning, but he took it back and gave it to our company commander, Captain Nesbitt (not his real name). The captain personally handwrote a reply and gave it to me to type. It was articulately and politically written. Although he did not apologize for the lack of her son's training, he told Mrs. Brown how brave Jake had been and how sorry his fellow marines were for her loss. He said that he had personally known Jake and asked her to continue to write him with further questions or correspondence. It was the last I heard from Mrs. Brown, and I do not know if she further communicated with the captain. I do know this: war should not be the place for on-the-job training!

I ultimately realized how consequential my position was to the men in Fox Company and their respective families. All soldiers deserve the awards they are entitled to, both heroically and meritoriously. Some of the awards were automatic as long as I did the paperwork. The loss of a limb or body part earned the Bronze Star, an exchange of gunfire with the enemy earned the participants the Combat V, and a wound from enemy fire or a booby trap was deserving of the Purple Heart. Other awards were submitted to battalion headquarters for approval and required an accurate written description of the marine's actions. Most marines in Fox Company soon knew my name. When they came into the rear, as they all did from time to time, some would stop in and ask, "Hey, Dave, did you get notice that I was in a firefight and should be put up for a Combat V?" I would always reply by looking up the paperwork and showing it to them. I was later written up and promoted by the company commander for positively boosting company morale by "diligently ensuring that all Marines received the medals they were entitled to while serving in a combat theater."

2.4. Drugs

During my time in the rear, I met Corporal Hines (not his real name), who was in charge of the base laundry. We both liked college football and would share newspaper articles from sports pages sent to us by our family members. After I had known him for a while, he opened up to me with a heart-wrenching story, weeping as he uttered the final words. He had been a squad leader for Fox Company when his squad had discovered a booby trap while on patrol. One of the procedures that we were taught to perform when finding a booby trap was to take cover and then detonate it with a grenade or a C-4 charge. However, after they had called it in, his lieutenant had told him to feign as if they were leaving the area and then double back and wait for the VC who had set it. This was also a procedure used in Vietnam since one of our jobs was to prevent future marine casualties. Most booby traps were set during the day and removed just before nightfall. The reason for this was that the enemy moved around at night and did not want to trip their mines. The squad returned and hid in a concealed area. Eventually, a VC appeared and began to remove the booby trap. The corporal moved his squad forward and called for the man to *dung lai* (Vietnamese for "Don't move!"). The VC chose to run, and the corporal shot him dead. He had just been a boy—estimated to be approximately twelve years old. Corporal Hines became a conscientious objector and his commanding officer brought him into the rear and placed him in charge of the base laundry.

Shooting a VC this age was not a common occurrence. This was the only time I heard of a marine taking direct aim at a child during my two years in the Marine Corps, other than occasional off-color humor. We were cautious to not intentionally shoot at children, women, or noncombatants. The boy looked older from a distance and in the near darkness of the late evening. Regardless of age, he was a VC who had set a booby trap in order to kill or injure US soldiers. However, it was understandable that Corporal Hines could not continue as a combat soldier. He told me that he knew that it was something he would have to live with.

Corporal Hines took me to a secret underground bunker one night that he had constructed under his laundry. We went through a normal bunker and then through a trapdoor in the floor and dropped down to a lower level with the help of a few ammo boxes. He had run an electrical wire from the base generator to power a psychedelic strobe light and a boom box, currently playing loud Jimi Hendrix music ("Purple Haze").[15] The entire room was so full of pot smoke that I could hardly make out any faces. I sat down along a wall, where I was passed a reefer. I took a puff and passed it on. There were about ten marines, all sitting along the sandbag walls. I recognized many of them, as my eyes adapted to the heavy haze in the room. I stayed for about a half hour and then climbed up the ammo boxes, pushed open the trapdoor, stumbled through the top bunker, and came out into the night. It was hot down there and hard to breathe with all the pot smoke and lack of good ventilation, although Corporal Hines had run one ventilation pipe. I was stoned from the thick secondary smoke, nearly blind from the strobe light, and wet and sweaty from the heat. The loud music caused my ears to ring throughout the next day. I never returned, but I kept the secret so no one would get into trouble. To my knowledge, authorities never discovered it.

Drugs were a problem in Vietnam, largely because they were an affliction in the United States. Drug abuse had cruelly ambushed our generation, and the easy availability of drugs in Southeast Asia made for a lethal combination for some of the soldiers in Vietnam. However, I believe that illegal drugs were used by a smaller percentage in Vietnam than by our generation stateside. We had officers and noncommissioned officers who policed us, and there were strict rules with harsh penalties if we were caught. I also believe that the military, similar to parents and authorities in the United States, was not prepared to deal with the vile outburst of illegal drug usage.

Illegal drug use was much more prevalent in the rear than in the bush. Most marines who smoked marijuana bought it in a "party pack," which cost ten dollars in MPCs. You could ask any local, including the kids, for a party pack, and they would have it for you in a matter of minutes. I seldom smoked pot and never bought any since the marines who did buy it were always eager to share.

I also knew two marines who were caught with party packs and sentenced to six months of in-country hard labor and given a dishonorable discharge afterward. I became acquainted with them when they returned from hard labor and came into our headquarters for their orders home. They seemed like normal guys and were noticeably embarrassed and ashamed of their fate. I could only imagine their parents' pain as each family had to face the reality of going from being proud of their marine and warrior to the humiliating reality of a drug-related dishonorable discharge. Afterward, I stayed clear of all drugs and distanced myself from the marines who used them. I had previously allowed peer pressure to overcome common sense, but I was now ready to break away from people and activities that could diminish my life's progress.

During my initial time in the bush as a grenadier, I could not help noticing our platoon radioman. He wore a bush hat instead of a helmet and carried a snub-nosed submachine gun instead of a government-issued M16. He said it was more suitable for jungle warfare, but it appeared to have come right out of a 1920s-era Chicago mob movie. It might have been an apt weapon for Al Capone and his boys (as used by Capone's thugs in the Saint Valentine's massacre), but it wasn't an effective weapon for Vietnam. Everyone knew him as Smokey Dog, a handle he used on the radio: "Fox Six, this is Smokey Dog, over."

Once transferred to the rear, Smokey Dog and I became good friends. He had been reassigned to Fox Company's base radio station, and his radio room was just ten feet from my desk. I learned that his "grease gun" was a .45-caliber submachine gun. In Vietnam, we seemed to have the liberty to vary from military standards. Smokey Dog was into his second tour and took advantage of a lot of these liberties. A major reason for this was that he was well liked, especially by the company commander. How could a lifer not like a marine who humped a radio and walked around the rice paddies and jungles wearing a bush hat and carrying a Mafia-style gun? Smokey Dog could have been an eccentric actor in a war movie.

Smokey Dog began leaving his radio room at night, asking me to man the radio. He normally stayed out until midnight or later and returned stoned out of his mind. Occasionally, he stayed in and other marines would come in and crowd into the small radio room—about ten by ten feet—and snort a white substance they said was heroin. While they were getting high, I typed awards from the other room while listening for radio calls from the bush. It was a way of being available if necessary, and it helped me stay on top of my duties as awards writer. One night, I detected a glue smell coming from the radio room. Smokey Dog was sniffing glue, which he said had been mailed to him from a buddy in the States. It appeared that he had soaked part of a rag with glue and lit it with a lighter, causing it to smoke. He would periodically place the smoldering rag inches from his face to sniff the smoke.

When Smokey Dog's tour was up, he returned to the world owing me one hundred dollars. I had unwisely loaned him the money, which he had said was to pay off a gambling debt, promising to reimburse me next payday. Later when I was stateside, I located him at his hometown in Florida and sent a letter asking to be paid (he gave me his address before he left Vietnam). I received a reply from his girlfriend saying that he was in prison for drug use, but he told her to tell me that I would get my money once he was released and working again. That was my last contact with him or his girlfriend, but I've always wished him well. Smokey Dog was a good guy and when he left our unit, it was the completion of his second tour in Vietnam. As I look back at these times, I was one of Smokey's enablers. He was a good soldier and would not have left his station or gotten that high if he knew he had to be sober enough to handle the home radio himself. I also bet my one hundred dollars went for drugs.

On one of the nights after Smokey Dog left Vietnam, I was listening to the chatter from the field on our base radio when the VC ambushed one of our squads attempting to pass a small grove of bamboo trees. A well-concealed and entrenched enemy attacked them with small arms fire and grenades. Two marines were seriously injured and required an emergency medevac. The VC vanished into the trees when the marines returned fire. It was unclear if any VC were hit. I recognized the voice of the radioman that was frantically calling for a medevac as PFC Anderson (I have forgotten his real name). We had become friends during basic infantry training at Camp Pendleton, California, and had arrived in country together. It was his first emergency medevac situation while under fire, and his voice revealed that he was obvious shaken by the surprise attack, but I was impressed by how he professionally handled all facets of his duties that night. PFC Anderson's ability to accurately notify his command of the casualties, call in the medevac, and also call for illumination rounds from our firebase was an inspiration to me that I called upon later when as a squad leader, I needed to react as he did.

2.5. Papa Haas

One of the marines I spent time with in the bush, Lance Corporal Hastens (Papa Haas) was from Columbus, Ohio (Hastens was not his real name). We became good friends by sharing fond memories of our hometown and bullshitting about the best pickup bars. He was a large, stocky, former high-school wrestler and liked to take on a half dozen local soldiers at the same time. The Popular Forces (PFs) often camped with us so that we could teach them to defend their country when we eventually left. Of course, this was somebody's political idea (called "Vietnamization"), and it did not have a chance of succeeding. Most of the PFs were boys, eighteen years old or younger, and the rest were older farmers. It was difficult for us to take them seriously, but I thought it was more difficult for them to take themselves serious enough to someday be our replacements.

Papa Haas must have thought that they should learn to wrestle in order to be good combatants. It was hilarious to watch him throw these little guys (all of them less than a hundred pounds) around, as they would try to get him down by sneaking behind him or jumping on him in a half-assed coordinated attack. Of course, it was all for fun, and everyone laughed as the little fellows finally conceded—usually one or two at a time from exhaustion. As an enticement to wrestle the Papa Haas, he would reward them with some C rations (we would help by contributing some of ours). He became their favorite marine. They would say, "Papa Haas boo-coo number one marine." They were fond of him because of his size, funny personality, and the special attention he gave them. No other marine was same-same to Papa Haas.

Earlier marines had spread a rumor to the PFs that in order to qualify to be a US Marine, you had to kill your mother to confirm your meanness. One day, I saw

Hastens weeping with an entire squad of PFs surrounding him. He looked up and screamed, "I kill mama-san" as they patted him on the back and tried to console him.

The PFs were quiet but fun and not too serious about their role, contrary to what might be expected for young men growing up in a war zone. Since many had been recruited from rice villages, where they had been raised as farmers, they did not compare to many American soldiers, who had grown up playing organized team sports, hunting game, and participating in the Boy Scouts. We were not teachers and probably not good examples much of the time. They were naïve enough to believe we had all killed our own mothers. I could not imagine these kid soldiers in a firefight, and I sometimes wonder if any of them made it through the next four years alive. Unfortunately, if they did live, the harsh wrath of the victors awaited them.

Lance Corporal Hastens was in the rear one day, after I was transferred to awards writer, when he approached me and asked, "Dave, did you put me up for the Medal of Honor?" Even though I thought he was joking, I kept a straight face—to play along—and asked him why. My job was to write up awards for everyone deserving of one when it was submitted by his commanding officer. He claimed to have heroically jumped on, and covered with his body, an incoming enemy grenade to protect his fellow marines. I had been made aware of the incident he was referring to. Grenades had been thrown into his unit's perimeter wounding four Marines. When I asked him why he wasn't in multiple pieces rather than standing there, he said that the enemy's grenade that he jumped on had happened to be a dud. That was when I chuckled, not being able to hold it in any longer, and told him I would get on it as soon as his company commander sent it in. I never heard any more about it. Hastens remains the best bullshitter of all time. I should have written him up for a coveted "BS medal."

Note: The PFs and the RFs (Regional Forces) were hard for us to distinguish between. We referred to all of them as PFs. They often camped and patrolled on their own as evidenced by the frequent number of booby traps they tripped. Our choppers medevaced the PFs and RFs when they were injured—until the day US troops pulled out and left them to fight their own war.

2.6 The Marble Mountains and China Beach

While I was serving as awards clerk, a close buddy I had met in boot camp, Dave Hansen, surprised me by appearing at our base one weekend. He was stationed just outside Camp Lauer (my base), at the foot of the Marble Mountains. Dave was assigned to a Marine Corps Combined Action Program (CAP) unit that was to befriend, protect, and aid the people in a nearby hamlet. We began to hang out some weekends and visit the city of Da Nang on occasion. They offered all types of assistance, including militarily protecting the people in the village from the VC and giving them medical aid. The CAP corpsman performed medical aid for illnesses, wounds, and most other conditions. The CAP unit would medevac seriously ill or wounded civilians to the US Da Nang hospital. The village children became attached to the CAP marines and vice versa. On one of my visits, I helped them assemble a swing set for the kids of the village. I will always remember how thrilled they were, and also how polite—taking turns on the swings without quarrel. These kids enjoyed watching their playmates swing while waiting for their own turns. The CAP program was an effective one. Most CAP marines learned to speak Vietnamese as they protected and aided the people in their assigned hamlets.

One weekend day, Dave and I decided to climb to the top of one of the Marble Mountains. We had no reason or authority to do so, but why not? We took our M16s and the normal load of eight magazines of ammo with us. There were at least a dozen caves, some with large openings and others with smaller ones, which we entered by kneeling. The caves opened into temples, where we observed Buddhist monks on their knees with their heads down, quietly worshiping Buddha statues, some the size of a baby and others six- to eight-feet tall. Once we reached near the peak, we were able to see the South China Sea, our marine base, helicopters as they flew below us, and villages. It was a spectacular view in all directions.

It started to get late in the afternoon and we were concerned that the VC might be waiting for us on the way back, so we took a different path down the mountain. It was later discovered that the VC had a field hospital on Marble Mountain that concealed two thousand patients and troops. However, the sacred temples in the areas we visited seemed peaceful and off-limits to hostility on both sides.

Our trail down led us to the backside of the village, where a boy approximately two years young, with no legs from above his knees, was sitting on a tree stump. Corporal Hansen said that he had lost his legs from an explosion, but he was not sure whether it was from an enemy's blast or ours since it had happened before his arrival in country. It undoubtedly made no difference to the little boy. Some other children were running in a circle around the child as he laughed and moved his arms up and down in delight. Although it was good to see the little boy happy at that moment in time, he exhibited one of war's cruelest tragedies.

Note. There are no accurate records of the number of South Vietnamese civilians seriously wounded during the war, including amputees.[16]

Life in the rear was certainly different than I had experienced in the bush. On occasion, the beach that boarded the eastern part of Camp Lauer was open for our use. We had razor wire that encircled our camp, but there was a path where each strand of wire was fastened with homemade hooks that simply detached, enabling us to leave our compound for the beach (the gooks never found this one). I loved to bodysurf through the small waves and follow schools of fish underwater. There were a lot of local fishermen with small boats and nets in Vietnam, but this section of their South China Sea was off-limits. Since there were a lot of different types of fish (swimming in large and small schools) we felt that they instinctively knew to stay in our area.

I had visited most of the nearby beaches while stationed in Southern California, including beaches in San Clemente, Oceanside, Laguna Beach, Huntington, Santa Monica, and Newport, but the white sand and pure barren innocence of China Beach made it a different type of paradise. Prior to my deployment, a marine told me that you could see topless mermaids in the early morning sitting on the sand with their fins in the water. That was one story that I really wanted to believe.

One weekend day, while I was bodysurfing, a Bell AH-1 Cobra helicopter gunship flew in and started firing into the water about five hundred meters from shore. I was told they were shooting at sharks, but I believe they were just target practicing. The Cobra was our most-used deadly weapon, with various armaments including missiles and a three-barrel Gatling-style machine gun at its nose capable of firing 1,500 rounds per minute.[17] As it fired into the ocean from its Gatling gun, I experienced this incredible and intimidating part of our war power. The Cobra made several passes, coming in fast, firing into the sea, banking to its right, and quickly climbing to a high altitude before vanishing as swiftly as it had appeared.

2.7. The Rat Dude

Rats were an ongoing problem in the rear, and each barracks was issued rattraps. We would start to see the rats sneaking around outside just as it began to get dark each night. Once we fell asleep, they would come into our barracks and eat the food we had lying around. I earned the title of our barrack's "rat dude" for catching the most rats, and it was a title I was proud of. My secret was the cheese I would take from the mess hall. Also, I would set my trap close enough to wake me when a rat tripped it. This way, I could remove the dead rat and set it again and again. Catching rats was good entertainment. In the morning, we would display the dead rats like trophies, hanging them by their tails on the clotheslines that ran along the fronts of our barracks.

If bitten by a rat, a soldier had to undergo two weeks of rabies shots in his belly. Hungry rats especially liked toes, and marines in heavily rat-infested areas would sleep with boots on to protect their toes from being gnawed on by these hungry varmints. The Vietnamese considered rat meat a delicacy and even served it in some restaurants on a stick (a rat kabob).[18] We would just bury ours later in the day.

Part III

★★★

3.1. COMBAT SQUAD LEADER

My time in the rear as an awards writer was challenging, but I had a burning desire to return to the bush. I had volunteered for Vietnam to hunt gooks, not type letters. It was the primary reason that I left college to join the marines.

We had experienced changes in leadership positions, and there was a lot of discontent in the rear, including a racial incident. There were daily problems at the chow line with mostly black marines who cut in front of others rather than starting at the rear of the line as they came to eat. One day, a few non-black marines tried to stop some of the black marines from cutting the line (they are referred to as non-black because they were Caucasian and Hispanic, and one was from a Caribbean island). A fight broke out, and marines from both sides were disciplined. Later that night, someone fragged the mess hall. An unknown person tossed an American M67 grenade into the seating area after everyone left. No one was hurt, but the problems in the rear were escalating, and morale was awful. Soon thereafter, a new in-country staff sergeant cornered me and wanted to know why my boots were not shined as he ruthlessly scolded me. He was right—my boots needed to be shined, but so did everyone else's. We were in a war zone. I had learned stateside that once a lifer noncommissioned officer (NCO) targets you, he would continue to do so. I faced a tough choice: buy or borrow some shoe polish or request a transfer and return to combat.

At about the same time that I requested a return to the bush, a call came in for a scout sniper, needed in our sniper battalion. I was the only certified sniper in our company and was ordered to exchange my M16 for a Remington 700 sniper rifle with a high-powered scope. My early days of hunting with my dad and grandfather, and later with my brother and our friends, had paid off on the rifle range in boot camp. I shot a score that qualified me as an expert, the highest grade possible. I was sent to Scout Sniper School immediately after Infantry Training Regiment, where I also qualified as an expert. I was excited about my new opportunity and was prepared to leave the next morning when I was told to wait a day because my orders were changing again. I was to go to a Fox Company platoon to take over a squad that had just lost its squad leader. I went to supply and exchanged my Remington 700 for an M16. The following day, I took a supply chopper and disembarked in a dry section of a rice paddy surrounded by mountains on three sides.

I became a combat squad leader after only forty-five days of prior experience in the bush, back when I was my squad's grenadier. However, I felt that I had gained a lot of wartime knowledge from my time as awards writer and overall time in country. At nearly twenty-one years of age, I was one of the older soldiers. I knew of many of the hot spots where we had hit booby traps or had gotten fired upon because I had written awards for marines involved in many of these incidents. The many nights of listening on the radio had taught me other tidbits of marine life in the bush and how to deal with them. Even though I had not been out for very long, I had served and learned under a proficient squad leader who had dealt with some unfortunate incidents that had resulted in the loss of four of his men. He had learned some hard lessons and thus displayed excellent leadership, caution, and communication abilities. I was proficient at reading and following topographic maps without man-made features (taught diligently in Scout Sniper School) and was confident I could handle the job. However, I was not prepared for the mess I was about to inherit once I ducked under the blades of the chopper and walked toward the center of the perimeter, where I met a young platoon commander, Second Lieutenant Novel (not his real name).

I was now a squad leader in a war zone—an equal to my TV hero, Sergeant Saunders in *Combat!* But that was the only similarity. I was a corporal, not a sergeant, and a newly promoted one at that. Unlike all stripes below it, a corporal stripe is supposed to transform a soldier into a leader. He or she is an NCO whom all lower ranks must obey. Transformation into true leadership usually happens over time, but model leadership development intended for stateside-premeditated timelines is not always possible in war. It was pertinent that I shortcut the learning curve. I received no leadership classes and no directives. It was as if I had been dropped from an airplane into a war zone without a parachute. I was escorted to my men by the platoon radioman, which I knew from previous meetings in the rear. Before he left me, he said, "Good luck. This is the worst squad in Vietnam."

My squad was at full strength, with thirteen men, including me. I was given a map of South Vietnam and a small book with blank pages that was to be my squad book for my men's personal information, notes, and our mission coordinates. I introduced myself to everyone, and on individual pages I wrote each man's full name, serial number, military occupation specialty, rank and date he was last promoted, rotation tour date, hometown, his M16 or weapon number, and his blood type (placed at the top of his page in large print). A few of the men did not want to give me their personal information, but I explained that I needed it for future promotion purposes. One marine said out loud, "He wants our blood type because he plans on getting us all shot up."

Now that I had everyone's information, it was time to assign duties according to rank status. The squad seemed to be in disarray, with hardly any assigned responsibilities. We had a point man and grenadier, but the radio operator had recently left for another squad, and there were no assigned team leaders. I asked for a volunteer to carry the radio, and only one man said, "I'll do it." He was a tall, thin, redheaded Irishman with a boyish smile named Les Fitzgerald (soon to be known as Fitz). Since humping the field radio was one of the toughest and most dangerous jobs in the bush, I was fortunate that Fitz volunteered because I would have had trouble assigning this position.

I next attempted to appoint the first, second, and third team leaders according to their rank as I had recorded in my squad book. The obvious first team leader was Corporal Carr (not his real name), who had seniority on me but had previously refused to be the squad leader. He immediately refused to be first team leader, a second-in-command position that would assume the duties of squad leader in the case of my death or a serious wound. Next in line was Lance Corporal Wheat (not his real name), our grenadier, who quickly accepted. Second team leader was Lance Corporal Tram (not his real name), and Corporal Carr, who had refused three higher positions, agreed to be the third team leader. We now had a chain of command, and everyone seemed satisfied with the appointments but remained unsure of me as the squad's leader.

Note: A corporal who refuses a leadership position could be disciplined and demoted to a lower rank for not demonstrating that he was worthy of being an NCO. Corporal Carr was never reported for refusing the squad leader position. He was a smart, analytical marine whom I relied on during my time as his squad leader, and he never tried to pull rank on me.

After two days back in the bush, I was assigned my first ambush patrol. My squad was already leery of my position as their leader, and I did not help my standing with them the first night. Most patrols had three to five coordinates that were mapped out in advance. The last coordinate was the final destination, and the others were checkpoints where we were to stop and call in on the radio. Our current point man was Buddy (not his real nickname), and the marine walking behind him was Lance Corporal Dim (not his real name). I walked third, with Fitz (the radioman) behind me. After about fifteen minutes, I stopped and told Fitz to call in checkpoint one. It was my first big mistake as a squad leader. I did not tell Buddy and Dim, the two men in front of me that we were stopping, so they kept walking—into the dark night by themselves and without any way to communicate. To further complicate the situation, our platoon commander, Lieutenant Novel, was a new-in-country and gung-ho second lieutenant and had anxiously asked to join us and go on his first ambush patrol (as the ranking soldier, he did not need to ask). When he heard me softly calling for the two lost marines, he came forward for an explanation. I told him that we had lost two men and that I was going to call our home base for permission to shoot a green flare in order to notify the lost men of our position, but he said we could not do that. I immediately realized that it would look bad on him, since he was the ranking marine and should have been the leader anyway. Therefore, we all wandered around in the night calling "Buddy?" and "Dim?"

After fifteen long, harrowing minutes, Dim came up behind me and tapped me on the shoulder, screaming, "Where the hell did you guys go?"

It took me a few minutes to calm him down and we moved on to our final coordinates. I placed the squad in a curved formation in a sandy bed of tall boulders.

The following day the second lieutenant congratulated me on a good job handling the situation and on the ambush. Most of my squad was still upset, but I realized later that most grunts in the bush are used to things not going right. Therefore, it was not as big a deal as I thought it to be (note: Fitz did not remember that we had lost two marines when we connected with each other years later). If I had been there for a while, it might have even been laughable. Nevertheless, I was upset with myself.

The following morning, Buddy and Dim approached me and said they no longer wanted to walk in the front of our squad. I asked for a volunteer for point man and, once again, had one volunteer. Fig (not his real nickname) was born in the Philippine Islands. He was an astute marine who was cognizant of our problems and always wanted to be part of the solution. I contacted our first sergeant (Top) in the rear for the dates of the next mine school. Fig was choppered out for special training just a day or so later and returned in three days to assume his new position.

There was a popular saying among grunts that the best way to judge a good point man, besides being lucky, is that he and everyone behind him comes home alive and in one piece. Fig turned out to be an excellent point man, always alert and constantly assessing the route and possible mined areas. In addition, he now had training on the types of mines, ways that the enemy used to set and mark them, and methods to find or avoid them.

Fig safely led us on every mission for the remainder of our tour together. He stopped at the checkpoints when he thought appropriate and continued a short time afterward. I no longer had to worry about losing anybody when stopping because I could trust our point man.

Fitz and Fig were pivotal in our future success as a rifle squad. They both volunteered to do dangerous and difficult jobs in a combat theater and then performed their duties with steadfast professionalism. Trading my awards-writer job in the rear for all this responsibility may be my all-time most reckless decision. I gave up a comfortable seat behind my typewriter, an occasional day at China Beach or the Marble Mountains, and my friends for a return to Vietnam's hell zone. I never gave it a second thought while I was back in the bush and have never regretted it. I only regret telling my family of my new duties at the time and adding more worry to their hell.

3.2. McNamara's 100,000 (per Year)

All marines must be physically and mentally strong!

—Sgt. Harris, drill instructor

By mid-1969, US infantrymen in Vietnam were battling an unexpected enemy in their own ranks: "shit birds." A good warrior is not just brave but disciplined. This requires the ability to listen and learn through the training period prior to deployment and a common sense that enables a person to synthesize his or her knowledge into practical use. Ideal requirements for combat preparedness include a sense of brotherhood along with an aptitude to have learned from both military classes and experiences as told by veteran soldiers. It requires the necessary intelligence to grasp, maintain, and deploy this knowledge when needed. When it comes to preparing for war, all instruction matters. Soldiers cannot pick and choose what lessons they may need to learn and what they are pretty sure they don't need (as might have been the case in high school). A soldier may not be a machine gunner by specialty but find himself in this position for a fallen brother while under fire. His life and others are now dependent on whether he listened and learned during as little as one machine gun class in Infantry Training Regiment, which all marines must attend after boot camp. Such classes teach machine gun basics—loading, operating, and how to clear a jam or affix the tripod. All marines are trained for combat, including cooks, office personnel, and members of the elite Marine Corps Band and Color Guard. When placed into a war zone, a person who cannot follow protocol, rebels against discipline, is not a team player, and has a serious inability to understand the causes and effects of his actions is a liability to himself and others around him.

Survival necessity alone cannot reverse a man's behavior, particularly if his conduct has been a personal limitation during his entire educational life. If he did not listen well in school and cannot employ imparted lessons, or if he lacks the aptitude to learn from parents, colleagues, and other mentors—as his peers did—he will likely be undesirable in the military as well as in many other professions. The armed forces have known for decades that those whose intellect falls below a predetermined level, along with a lack of basic discipline, do not make good soldiers. It is not just low intelligence that makes a soldier undesirable. Most people are not that far off from one another on the intellectual scale, and there certainly have not been many geniuses humping around in war zones, especially among the American troops who were in Vietnam. Historically, a recruit's eligibility to serve in the armed forces has partly been determined through test scores. Additionally, a recruit must meet the minimum requirements for age, physical and mental condition, and pass a criminal background check. During the Vietnam era, each recruit was rated by a category (I, II, III, IV, and V, with I being the highest).

Hamilton Gregory revealed (June 2015) the reason for all the military misfits during the Vietnam era in his book *McNamara's Folly: The Use of Low-IQ Troops in the Vietnam War, plus the Induction of Unfit Men, Criminals, and Misfits*. Gregory explains that Robert S. McNamara, as the secretary of defense under President Lyndon B.

Johnson and one of the most well-known names of the Vietnam War, lowered the armed forces entry standards as a way to get enough troops without drafting college students (student deferment, 2-S) and to continue to allow questionable medical deferments (unfit for military service, 4-F) to the sons of many middle-class families.[19] These were political decisions to protect the president from losing the vote of the middle-class demographic while satisfying the desperate need for soldiers by the armed forces.

Note: Some of the medical deferments declared by family doctors during the Vietnam War included flat feet, high arches, and chronic headaches.

When McNamara lowered the requirements to enter the armed services of the United States, he put all servicemen in danger. Many of these young men lacked the aptitude to be good warriors. They didn't listen or learn well, and they definitely did not take orders well. They were drafted or accepted into the armed services even though they tested below previously set minimal qualifications, and they were then placed into a combat theater without significant readiness, requiring them to learn on the job or by their own mistakes, including getting themselves or others hurt or killed. Imagine going to war with the kids who acted up and lacked discipline in high school classes. School was all about what they could get away with, not achieving knowledge. They disrespected their teachers, disrupted classes, and got failing or low grades. Many of them flunked or dropped out. Now, imagine these men carrying an automatic weapon alongside you in a war!

The reality (as I personally experienced) was they disrespected authority and were incapable of adhering to orders, talked aloud on covert ambushes, and wrongly influenced other soldiers. They did not listen or comprehend most of the teachings in training classes and thus had to be babysat on even the simplest tasks. Their entire lives, they had broken most of the rules and believed that procedures did not apply to them, especially when superiors were not looking and when they could get away with not adhering to them. This attitude made it difficult on their superiors, fellow soldiers, and themselves, but they were incapable of understanding this. They were not the people who could be assigned to operate the radio, walk point, or be a team leader. A combat squad was better off without them, even if it meant operating below normal strength. They really were shit birds.

I learned from being put in charge of Pete Trivette (not his real name) in boot camp that babysitting one of these men was a full-time job. Trivette, who was from Louisiana, could not comprehend even the simplest tasks. Our drill instructor (DI) appointed me to be responsible for "every waking and sleeping minute of shit-bird Trivette's life." The rules were simple: "Gerhardt, anything Trivette fucks up, you will both pay me for."

Along the way, in spite of the extra physical training I had to do because of him, Pete and I became friends. This was in part because I helped him write love letters to his girlfriend. I can still hear his drawl: "Hey, Dive, how do you spall *darlin'*?" In return, he shared some of her topless pictures she would mail to him.

One night, I heard that some of the other guys were going to give Trivette a "blanket party" sometime after dark. This was a marine way of handling the shit birds that caused others to do extra physical training and lose privileges. Each participant was to take a bar of soap, wrap it in a pillow case, sneak into our quarters, and cover Trivette's head with a blanket while they beat him with their brutal weapons. I slept in the bunk above him and unlocked my M14 rifle from the bed's railing and slept with it. I announced that I would give a vertical butt stroke to the head of anyone who approached our bunks. I meant it, and I believe everyone else knew it too, since no one approached our bunk that night. The next morning, I put my rifle back, but in my haste, did not fully engage the padlock. We went on a run, and when we returned, my rifle was missing, and the DI was walking around with an M14. It had to be mine—I just knew it, and I knew that I was going to be in big, big trouble. I approached the DI quarters after we were settled. "Sir, the private forgot to lock his rifle last night, sir."

DIs were predictable. "Why the hell did you even have it unlocked, you toilet-licking scumbag?"

DIs from three other platoons shared the same billet, but they did not seem to be interested in me—or the rifle problem---until they heard my reply. "Sir, the private slept with his rifle last night, sir."

"*Why the hell did you sleep with your rifle?*" he methodically screamed, now inches from my face. And then, sarcastically, "Did you think it was your girl?"

"No, sir. Some of the men were going to give Private Trivette a blanket party, and I warned them that I would vertical butt stroke anyone's head that approached our bunk, sir."

I continued to stand at attention while the other DIs stopped what they were doing as I felt their hard stares. I had prepared myself for just about anything except what happened next: my DI—the world's meanest man—unpredictably handed me my rifle and sternly said, "Get the hell out of my house!"

Notes: The vertical butt stroke was a maneuver we learned in close combat training. It was taught as a way to "jar the enemy's brains" by striking him with the butt of our rifle in an upward or downward motion.

After boot camp and Infantry Training Regiment, I lost contact with Pete. He was assigned a 0300 (infantry) classification and orders to Vietnam. His name is not on the Wall. I have always believed that this incident cost me the chance for my first promotion.

It was now a year after boot camp, and I was the leader of a rifle squad in Vietnam. At least four men in my squad were Pete Trivettes—on steroids. Bean, a thin marine from Louisiana, and Roadie, from the New England area, were the ringleaders and prime troublemakers. Their insubordination came to a sudden confrontational point approximately five or six days after I had assumed my new position. I was trying to organize the squad for an ambush patrol when they refused to join my squad briefing. These short meetings assured that everyone was on board with our mission, its location, enemy intel (if available), location of other squads, return route to our command post, rally point if we got separated, and permission-to-fire requirements. Even though it seemed like a trivial incident, it was obvious that these two picked this time to defy my authority in front of the other members of our squad. In addition to their insubordination, I could not leave on patrol and set up an ambush without knowing that all members fully understood our mission. Abruptly, the full attentiveness of everyone in the squad was on me, and I knew that I had to stay strong. I approached Bean and sternly said, "Either obey the order, or I will write you both up." The Marine Corps took insubordination seriously, and everyone knew that he had better not get written up for disobeying a lawful order from an NCO, especially during wartime. I knew that I was in trouble either way—between a rock and a hard place. I was standing inside our platoon's perimeter in Vietnam, surrounded by the other men in my squad—with no support from any superiors and facing two angry men. I could not back down, but I gave them one more chance. "Last warning. I'll write you up if you do not come join us, but if you do come, I'll forget this whole matter."

Bean and Roadie were also in the middle. They were in front of their friends and were evidently the badass leaders of what had become the squad's defiant faction. They both replied as they walked away, "Yeah, well, fuck you!"

I was still in my first few days as squad leader and found myself doing something I never thought I would do—writing up two of my men. I had naïvely presumed that we would all be friends and that everyone would follow my lead. I wrote about the incident in my little green memoranda book, removed the finished papers, and handed them to the second lieutenant, who sent the write-ups into the rear on the next supply chopper. A few days later, Captain Nesbitt arrived in a private chopper and held company office hours for Bean and Roadie next to their foxholes. They each received a fine and lost one rank. I felt bad for both of them but did not show it. By standing up to Bean and Roadie, I had established that I was in charge. The tail no longer wagged the dog in this squad. I still do not look at it as a strong leadership moment but rather as a desperate decision with no other viable choice. My writing up Bean and Roadie in the first week of my authority established some discipline. The necessity of having to unwaveringly follow my orders would later save the lives of these two marines—on at least two separate occasions.

I was experiencing the degeneration of the armed forces but thought it to be a normal military life, not realizing that our secretary of defense had created the mess by introducing hundreds of thousands of previously unqualified men into the ranks of the armed forces. As a combat squad leader, I became more of a babysitter than a leader, wasting too much valuable time and resources on "Gerhardt's misfits" (as they became known to other squad leaders). For example, most of the members of our squad (except the grenadier) carried an M16 rifle. The M16 had some earlier problems of jamming during firefights. Some of the difficulties were identified as a lack of preventive maintenance. We were taught how to disassemble and clean our rifles in stateside training and were issued gun-cleaning kits in Vietnam. Our weapons were exposed to the elements twenty-four hours a day, seven days a week. This included dirt, rain, humidity, rust, and insects that would crawl inside the barrel or into other parts. In our cleaning kits was a small container of oil that we were to use on the moving parts and put on the springs in our magazines to keep them from rusting and jamming. Although it made clear sense to keep our weapons and magazines clean and oiled, the problem soldiers (as I refer to them now) in our squad would not take care of their rifles. On occasion, some of the rifles looked so bad that I had to demand that these marines clean them. At times, other members of our squad (especially Fig) helped them or cleaned their rifles for them.

Another example of irresponsible behavior was our weekly antimalarial pill. It was a large tablet that no one enjoyed swallowing, but it was required for the purpose of preventing malaria. I would normally have to demand that my problem soldiers take their pills (dispatched by the corpsman), especially in the first month of my authority, reminding them that they could be disciplined if they contracted malaria. Some would reply that it could also be their ticket home.

For whatever reasons, my problem soldiers could not correlate their future well-being with their regular behavior and habits. Someone else had to do this for them. Another example was encouraging them to have proper foot hygiene so that they would not contract what bush soldiers in Vietnam called "toe rot." The correct terminology was "immersion foot," but it was sometimes referred to as "jungle rot." Perpetual wet boots from humping through rice paddies or rivers or sweaty socks from the high humidity were its primary causes. Immersion-foot symptoms included the toes and surrounding area of the feet turning an ugly black-and-reddish color. Sometimes, the bottoms of the feet showed cracking and bleeding. The marines who came down with it told me that it was very painful, especially during long hikes. Often, they had to be medevaced to the rear. It was important that we removed our boots as often as possible—at least once per day—to allow them to dry out. We were supposed to carry extra pairs of dry socks and wash and dry the dirty ones. We also scrubbed our feet with soap and canteen water when not near a river where we could bathe. Toe rot was a common problem during the monsoon season, but with good hygiene, it was not that difficult to avoid at other times.

A last example of my babysitting: although it was not my rule, I told the squad that in accord with our platoon commander's orders, boom-boom girls were off-limits. I had to keep an eye on Roadie for this one.

The problem members of my squad were hyperactive men who knew rebellion but not adherence. They were a leader's nightmare as they disobeyed and ignored nearly all directives. It was rumored that some of the men had felony records, but this was never proven. Although their disobedience was usually not blatant, it was clearly insubordinate. They were so vocal that their thoughts always came out without a filter, and this, combined with their negative attitudes and disrespect for authority, caused problematic disruptions. The constant bitching would fuel others, especially the soldiers with negative outlooks on the war or any one-day mission. There were other "Bean followers" in our squad, along with one marine from another squad who hung out with them when we were idle during the daytime. They had not yet learned the concept of team success or developed a cooperative aptitude beyond their own self-importance.

It is difficult to understand how any soldier could not take his placement in a war zone seriously, but some men lacked the resilience to timely acclimate to change. The lack of conformity (including taking orders), excessive drinking, drug use, loud show-off behavior, sneaking off to find boom-boom girls, and smoking and talking on night ambushes were all examples of their unruliness. The responsible members of our squad helped me babysit these problem soldiers and prevent any *perceived* dangers. These misfits changed the scenery of the Marine Corps more than the corps changed them. The old adage "Join the service, and they will make a man out of you" is not applicable to all.

Predictably, what temporarily shut them up was engagement with the enemy or an ill-fated incident such as a comrade hitting a booby trap. A good firefight or an unfortunate land-mine detonation where fellow soldiers were injured served as hard knocks teachings. When on patrol, they were placed in line from the middle back, but not last. A squad's "tail-end Charlie" was a key position that guarded movement from behind and watched over the squad as we moved forward. Other primary and responsible positions were the radioman (always next to the squad leader), grenadier, and the first, second, and third team leaders. However, all members of a squad are an important link and must be professionally prepared for the possibilities of danger, tragedy, and even the need for them to take a leadership role.

Fast-forward forty-four years: I found a Les Fitzgerald in Washington State, where my green memorandum book that I carried in Vietnam said he was from. It was Fitz! We talked for hours and shared some missing links with some of the incidents we remembered. He told me that I was a replacement for Sergeant Bleu (not his real name), who had been hit by a sniper's bullet. Sergeant Bleu had fallen on Fitz, who had helped him to the ground while they awaited the corpsman. Fitz also told me that the day Sergeant Bleu had been hit, they had not been able to find the platoon commander, a second lieutenant who had recently joined the Fox platoon, but a few of the marines had known where he was. They had gone to a boom-boom girl's pup tent to fetch him.

I later made my first visit to see Fitz. We exchanged photos, and he told me the story surrounding the camera that he had taken his pictures with. He had bought it for five dollars from Roadie so that Roadie could visit the same boom-boom girl, just before the second lieutenant's visit, on that fateful day that Sergeant Bleu had been shot. That was when I decided I must write this book.

The sheer numbers of McNamara's misfits into the armed forces' ranks countered discipline and turned bases and field units into chaos. The fear of being fragged kept the brass from enforcing strict guidelines that all militaries have required since the historical beginnings of warfare. This lack of discipline in Vietnam resulted in low morale among all the troops, along with everything bad and nothing good. It also had a lasting effect on the armed forces as good soldiers refused to re-up when their current tour of duty expired.

Notes: Some final facts concerning McNamara's experiments with America's young men:

McNamara labeled his program Project 100,000, after the number of below-standards men he wanted to induct each year. There were 354,000 total below-standards men taken into the armed services by the end of the Vietnam War. Their fatality rate was three times that of other GIs.[20] One Project 100,000 man inducted had an IQ of sixty-nine and was fourteen years old when he completed the third grade.[21]

The most striking statistic: more than 50 percent of the 354,000 Project 100,000 men received a discharge other than honorable.[22] Not only does this prove the failure of this program and reveal the natures of more than half of these men, but it made it difficult for them to get meaningful jobs and made it more likely that they would become homeless, dangerous, and burdens on society.

It was also labeled the New Standards Program by the armed forces. The following statistics are stunning:[23]

Armed forces qualification, medium percentile score:

New standard men = 13.6 percent

Regular recruits = 56.8 percent

Prior-service civil court convictions:

New standard men = 9.2 percent

Regular recruits = N/A

(9.2 percent of 354,000 = 32,568 men with civil court convictions entering into the ranks of the armed forces)

"One of the single biggest blunders of our Vietnam experience," said Lieutenant Colonel Charles L. Armstrong of the Marine Corps, "was the Project 100,000 folly of taking on board marginally qualified individuals under the mistaken watchword of 'infantry doesn't have to be real smart.' Dumb Grunt, however, is not a

complete phrase—Dumb Dead Grunt is. You don't have to be a Fulbright Scholar to be a good rifleman, but you can't be stupid."[24]

3.3. First Lieutenant Timberlake

Fox Company was going through platoon commanders as fast as any other position. By design in Vietnam, the platoon commander was normally a second lieutenant fresh out of Officer Candidate School in Quantico, Virginia. They were first assigned combat duty in the bush for six months and then moved to the rear as the company executive officer, supply officer, intelligence officer, or other rear duty. Somewhere in that time, they were promoted to first lieutenant. The six months out and six months in were designed to get more officers combat experience, but it also removed officers from their field units just as they were becoming proficient as wartime leaders.[25] In other words, by replacing field commanders every six months with boot lieutenants, the military high command was using Vietnam as officer training pants in preparation for a real war.

When I first arrived in country, one of Fox Company's best platoon commanders was Lieutenant Perra, who had been wounded in the leg while on patrol, but was able to return to his unit soon afterwards. He was made our executive officer after six months of combat duty. When I returned to the bush, the second lieutenant (name unknown) who was reported to be in a boom-boom girl's pup tent when Sergeant Bleu was shot had just been relieved of his duties. The presumption was that the officer was replaced for lack of leadership; including being a poor example—as evidenced when he was caught with his pants down during an emergency medevac. In addition, he was in trouble for gambling with enlisted men and taking $800 from them in one night. Second Lieutenant Novel, fresh out of Officer Candidate

School, replaced him and became our platoon commander. He was a nice, soft-spoken leader who was obviously trying to pretend that he knew enough to take control and make decisions rather than ask for others' advice. Normally, proper guidance would come from the platoon sergeant, but ours (Sergeant Beck) greatly lacked any type of leadership aptitude.

One night, while we were set in our ambush site, a man's voice started yelling, "*Chieu hoi, chieu hoi.*" It was obvious to me that there was a VC who wanted to surrender. I estimated that he was approximately a hundred meters away and yelling in all directions. I was excited about capturing a POW, even if it was a non-combat surrender. I called the platoon radioman and reported it, not knowing whether we should move toward the voice or confirm the surrender and yell back to "*lai di*" ("come here"). Our platoon radioman said that our platoon commander, Second Lieutenant Novel, wanted us to move forward and capture him. As we were preparing to move toward the area where the voice was coming from, Captain Nesbitt—who had been monitoring the radio calls—intercepted and told me to "ignore it." He added, "If he wants to *chieu hoi*, he can do so in daylight." No one surrendered the next day. It had been an obvious ploy to lure us into an ambush or have us expose our position. Captain Nesbitt, who was on his second tour in Vietnam, had wisely protected our squad from falling for a VC trap when he overruled the boot lieutenant.

As a new squad leader, I lacked two key qualities:

First, I was a new NCO and lacked the necessary leadership ability.

Second, I had only minimal field experience. Like many other Vietnam leaders, I was rushed into my new position. Due to the high turnover of personnel, quickly promoted officers and NCOs were commanding troops in a war zone before they were ready. None of my immediate superiors, including our platoon sergeant and platoon commander, was the type of leader who was capable of any type of effective guidance. A lack of leadership development of field personnel and an anemic concern by the high command to seriously address it put the burden on raw individuals attempting to fill vitally important positions. I had to learn fast and without a mentor. The placement of boot platoon leaders fresh out of Officer Candidate School (and their removal after only six months), unfit lifers serving as platoon sergeants, new NCOs as squad leaders (like me), and the addition of "McNamara's misfits" was similar to the blind leading the blind leading the blind leading the incompetent. Some platoon commanders, platoon sergeants, and squad leaders lacked experience or leadership, and some platoon sergeants were stupid. This was true with Staff Sergeant Beck, our platoon sergeant. He was a danger to other marines for reasons that I will expound on later.

Qualified leaders—at all levels in a combat theater—are essential to success, and perhaps even the lives or deaths of the soldiers who were dependent on their leadership and decisions. The vast majority of battles in Vietnam were small, squad-sized firefights and ambushes. A squad leader's skills must include the ability to read and follow coordinates on a map and not get his squad lost. There are no street signs in rice paddies, jungles, and mountains. He must have the ability to accurately call for fire support using his map's coordinates, which can be a savior when a superior force confronts his squad. Combat experience, knowledge of the enemy's tactics and past successes, assuredness of his squad's combat readiness, and the abilities to anticipate problems and protect his squad from harm (such as land mines) should be some of the tested requisites. Additionally, the squad leader position requires knowledge to make both routine and grave decisions, including being militarily and combat astute and exercising resolved control of the men he is responsible for.

As a junior squad leader in Vietnam, I was not prepared for the enormous number of problem soldiers assigned to my squad. Negative people oppose just about everything, including common-sense decisions, and ignorant people who did not learn their lessons during training (for a number of reasons) resist the practices of the leaders who did learn. It was difficult to fight a war beside soldiers who disobeyed authority. If a combat unit was fortunate enough to never hit a booby trap or never engage in a firefight with the enemy, it would still be in danger due to the ineptness of accident-prone shit birds carrying loaded weapons.

I felt confident that I could do the job, but since there was a lack of solid leadership above me to emulate, I was on my own and making mistakes. For example, I was afraid to say too much or over communicate with my men for fear I would be belittled and criticized—and ultimately not respected. What I did not realize is that small, squad-sized leadership decisions during wartime are often questioned by the squad's individual members regardless of rank. However, I felt that there was no one capable of doing a better job and that the most critical squad members were the least qualified to lead anyone.

Miraculously, Second Lieutenant Novel left on the supply chopper one afternoon as First Lieutenant Timberlake disembarked. No one was sure why Lieutenant Timberlake replaced a second lieutenant who had recently started his tour, but the second lieutenant was spotted in the rear getting on a jeep, never to be seen again. We were a platoon that had a rough history of problems, including unnecessary and even stupid accidents, and Lieutenant Timberlake had become available. He was on his second tour in Vietnam, having spent his first one as an infantry NCO. In our language, he had been a grunt like us. Prior to joining us in the bush, Lieutenant Timberlake did his homework and had viewed our files. In our initial meeting, he revealed that he knew I had attended Ohio State University, and that I was also a scout sniper. He somehow knew of the problems with some of the members of my squad, possibly from the prior office hours that Bean and Roadie had received when I wrote them up (my handwritten reports would have been in their respective files). The armed forces want leaders who are strict. Although I was unaware of it at the time, disciplining two of my men had given me extra credibility with the brass.

Lieutenant Timberlake also seemed to be friends with our company commander, Captain Nesbit, who was well aware of problems in our platoon, including the weakness of our platoon sergeant. It would be impossible to be around Staff Sergeant Beck for more than two minutes and not know that we had an exceedingly weak and pathetically stupid platoon sergeant. So here he was, First Lieutenant Timberlake, to save us from ourselves and win the war.

Once Lieutenant Timberlake assumed command of our platoon, I had someone to emulate—a mentor. He had a confident and firm manner that commanded respect from his men. In an initial meeting with the platoon, he explained that he would support his squad leaders and their decisions. Since this was his second tour in Vietnam, there was no learning curve or reason to act pretentious. I found myself explaining the nightly mission or sharing other knowledge with my men very similar to the way he briefed me and the other squad leaders. This gave me confidence as I grew into the job. Similar to Lieutenant Timberlake, I would say something just once, with authority and with the expectation that it would be followed. I no longer cared if anyone liked me or that I might be viewed as a big prick. This new attitude was more important in commanding respect than my superior stripe or stripes, which some squad members did not respect anyway. I learned to ignore the bitching (not the defiance) that usually followed a meeting or an order, especially when from the same men. Men with lower ranks sometimes referred to NCOs as "flies" because they "eat shit and bother people." I now understood why we bothered people (I never understood the other). Of utmost importance was the responsibility for everyone's safety, and that demanded solid leadership and good decisions, regardless of others' thoughts. For example, a leader may not want to confront a soldier over a matter, choosing to take the weak route and ignore it, but when it could cost lives, he has no choice. After one is forced by circumstances to be more of a leader, it becomes easier to do so.

One example of combat knowledge, or lack thereof, was the daily practice of moving our perimeter. Second Lieutenant Novel thought we should move our compound just before dark so we could see where we were going. The proper marine procedure was to move after dark so the enemy could not see where we were going or that we had moved. Once Lieutenant Timberlake took command, we always moved just after dark. One night the enemy heavily mortared our old location, obviously believing we were still there. Our policy of moving our position—after dark—proved to be a smart one, even saving lives. The incident reinforced the importance of this maneuver, but then every tactic had its importance.

3.4. First Lieutenant Perra and Tripping the Booby Trap

On March 21, 1971 Lieutenant Perra, the Fox Company executive officer, tripped a booby trap while returning to his jeep. This horrifying and avoidable event encompassed American habits and behaviors, the bravery and proficiency of American soldiers who performed the responsible jobs, and the idiocy of the incompetent ones who caused more problems than they resolved.

The day prior, our platoon was issued an experimental new product we called "feelers." They were simple antennas, approximately three feet tall that were to be stuck in the ground outside our perimeter. Each came with a battery-operated sensor that made a static sound if something came near it. My squad was issued three sets, but Staff Sergeant Beck did not want us to set them, claiming they were just another stupid idea from a civilian longhair who had never fought in a war. I considered them to be a good idea and told him a little white lie—that we had instructions from the company commander to try them. Fitz and I scattered them on our side of the perimeter approximately thirty meters from our position, camouflaged in knee-high grass.

At approximately 2300 that night, when I was on watch, one of the three antennas began sending static back to our sensor. All three had some occasional light static due to wind, but this one had obviously increased. I called our platoon radioman, and he awoke Staff Sergeant Beck, who was upset that I had bothered him. He told the radioman to tell me to ignore it. Shortly thereafter, the static on that censor ceased, but then a second one began, louder than the first one. I called back to the platoon radioman to alert them that "something's out there."

Staff Sergeant Beck got on the radio and was furious, again telling me to "ignore it." The static continued for about twenty minutes and then subsided. During that time, I called the platoon radioman to report it one more time, stating that I was going to shoot sunshine (illumination flares) over the area. Staff Sergeant Beck angrily stopped me once again.

The following morning, Lieutenant Timberlake approached me and said he and Staff Sergeant Beck had to go to the rear and that I was to take charge of the platoon. It was a little unusual in that I was not the senior NCO left behind. There was a rumor that Staff Sergeant Beck was being called in for a "talk" with the battalion commander concerning his behavior during past events. Some of the marines had written letters to our commander saying they believed that Staff Sergeant Beck was incompetent and a danger to the platoon. Every night he would light a cigar after dark, revealing our location, which we had inconspicuously moved to in order to prevent the enemy from finding us. The last straw was when our platoon was on a daytime patrol in a heavily mined area and he ordered a fire team (four men each) to walk on each of our flanks. This was a standard military maneuver, but it was not necessary in this situation, and it tripled the risk of tripping a booby trap. Several marines, including me, pointed out the danger of this maneuver, but he was too stubborn to change his mind. The teams started out as ordered, but they moved back in line shortly thereafter. Our survival instincts included not listening to the gobbledygook of an idiot. When he later saw that we were no longer on our flanks, he became furious and threatened to write us up for disobeying an order. This would have been difficult for him to do since he could hardly read and write. He later calmed down.

Prior to leaving for the rear with Staff Sergeant Beck, Lieutenant Timberlake gave me a direct order: "Don't let anyone go outside this compound." I thought that was also a strange request in that there was no place for anyone to go and the boom-boom girls knew better than to set up a pup tent outside Lieutenant Timberlake's platoon. However, I was sitting nearby when I spotted Bean and Roadie wandering down the path in front of me. My perimeter position was set up facing a footpath that led to a dirt road. I quickly jumped up and confronted my two men, telling them that they had to stay inside our perimeter. Naturally, they argued to the point of starting to walk away from me and down the path. I followed and threatened to report them if they disobeyed me. To my surprise, they returned to our perimeter, although I heard and ignored a "Fuck him," along with other expletives. My insistence that they not go any farther and return to their position, along with their decision to obey me, would later prove to save their lives.

Shortly afterward, Lieutenant Timberlake, along with our company executive officer, Lieutenant Perra, arrived by jeep to our compound. Lieutenant Perra had come to pass out payroll to the troops. After Perra distributed everyone's pay, he headed back toward the jeep, which was waiting on a dirt road five-hundred meters away. As he traveled down the path, I suddenly heard a loud and familiar explosion just twenty-five meters from my position. Lieutenant Perra had hit a booby trap made with an M26 (an American grenade) as he traveled on the footpath toward his jeep. As the smoke and dust began to clear, we could see the lieutenant sitting upright in a stunned, motionless state as a squad of men rushed towards him, including the platoon's corpsman, Doc Dew, and the company radioman, Corporal Stalzer.

I fell into line with the rescue squad as Stalzer dropped to one knee to change frequency and call in a medevac. He realized there was no need to waste time and go see the lieutenant's body first. The point man cautiously probed the ground with his probe stick as he neared the lieutenant. It was common practice for gooks to plant more than one booby trap, with the purpose of taking out the first responders while further injuring the soldier or soldiers hurt by the initial blast. Within two to three minutes of the explosion, Doc Dew was at Lieutenant Perra's side, administering first aid as he placed tourniquets to stop the profuse bleeding of his badly wounded legs and hand. While talking to the pilot on his radio, Corporal Stalzer walked the landing zone he had chosen, looking for additional mines and assuring level ground. As the chopper approached, he tossed a smoke grenade to signal our location. As it landed, Lieutenant Perra—now on a stretcher—was carried the short distance into the back of the CH-46 helicopter as its back door was lowering. The chopper left within twenty minutes of the explosion. The efficiency of the men involved in the lieutenant's medical treatment and medevac procedures was remarkable.

After the chopper left with Lieutenant Perra, Bean and Roadie told other marines in our platoon how lucky they were that they were not dead because they had been only a few steps from the booby trap when they turned around and went back into our perimeter. Of course, there was no mention of why they returned. Had I allowed them to continue down the path, they both would have been blown into a bloody mess, with their body parts strewn over the area, and they knew it. Lieutenant Perra was wearing a flak jacket, helmet, and boots. He was carrying an M16 whose stock took some of the shrapnel that would have hit his midsection. Bean and Roadie were wearing shorts and sandals and carrying walking sticks. The only reason they obeyed my command was because of my earlier discipline when I had written them up for refusing my direct orders.

I did not care or attempt to take credit for saving two of my marines' lives. I was really pissed at Staff Sergeant Beck for his inexcusable denial of movement in front of our position the night prior. It obviously was the enemy setting the booby trap that Perra hit. It was also obvious that the VC who had set the explosion were from the nearby village. I had unknowingly followed their movement from one sensor placed closer to the village to the second one, which was nearer the explosion.

We moved our position later that night without confronting them about the booby trap. I am still not sure what we were allowed to do. I knew that we needed permission and a Vietnamese interpreter to invade the village's perimeter and demand they turn over the men who had set the explosion, but not acting at all allowed them to get away with blowing up one of our guys and likely someday repeating this type of cowardly assault. Lieutenant Perra was a friend I knew from my previous duty as awards writer, when we sat next to each other in the Fox Company headquarters. I saw his mangled, bleeding body as we loaded him on the chopper and had this hollow feeling in my stomach that he had lost both of his legs and possibly an arm. Although this was an isolated incident, I understood the anger soldiers feel when a village aids and abets the enemy, resulting in buddies getting blown up or killed. Young men with guns and anger over lost comrades can become a recipe for retribution. The platoon commander and squad leaders (including me) would not have allowed any of our guys to enter the village. I do not believe any of the guys would have anyway.

After more rational thought regarding that ill-fated day, I began to consider possible feelings from the other side. We were camped in a cemetery—as we did on occasion. Our reasoning for this was that it was dry and safer than other places. The natives were not going to wake up their dead with a rocket attack on their relative's graves. We never desecrated the graves or markers, and there was no need to dig foxholes, which would mean digging down toward human remains. However, I am ashamed to admit that we dug small holes just outside our perimeter and at the edge of the cemetery to go to the bathroom (as we did in other locations). Additionally, it is impossible for fifty men to camp in a graveyard without some residual damage. Grave markers made great seats and backrests and were also good supports for our tents (we carried lightweight, camouflaged, quilted poncho liners for use as night coverings and daytime shelters from the sun).

The cemetery we were occupying undoubtedly contained the loved ones of the people in the hamlet that resided only three hundred meters away. I believe VC stationed or living in that hamlet set the booby trap that Lieutenant Perra detonated, as it was set on the hamlet side of the cemetery and in the direction from where the two sensors had revealed movement the night prior. Any of us would be upset to see a group of soldiers camped in our family's final resting place. However, the marines did not hold sensitivity classes—at least not during the Vietnam era. There is always going to be incidental damage, especially to personal property, in the homeland of a country at war. This includes bombed-out homes, smashed-in doors where forced entry is necessary, and damage to the land. Cemeteries, places of worship, and other sacred sites should remain untouched unless there is a real reason to enter them. Utilizing these types of safe havens can be self-defeating.

I now wonder how significantly our behaviors influenced locals and turned them against us. For example, I was a heavy smoker. Small cigarette packs were included in our C rations, and I supplemented mine with ones given to me by nonsmokers and from the BX store on the base (we could buy personal supplies that were brought to us by the supply chopper). I flicked a lot of cigarette butts into rice paddies, cemeteries, and wherever else we happened to camp without a second thought—until many years later when I became a landowner. I'm not very fond of people that trash my property, although I've never considered blowing their limbs off.

Fast-forward forty-six years: I located Paul Perra on the social website 'Together We Served." I had known Paul when he was a junior lieutenant with a heavily bandaged leg, limping around after he had been hit in the leg with shrapnel during a VC ambush. One of the other marines in his unit had died when he had caught a piece of shrapnel in his neck from the same attack. Lieutenant Perra had been medevaced to the Da Nang hospital and after healing had returned to the bush. He was later reassigned as the Fox Company executive officer when I was the awards writer. We had become friends and had respected each other's position in the company. When I later returned to the bush, I had been closest to Paul when he had tripped the booby trap. I have had a guilty feeling throughout all the years because I have always thought I could have prevented it by taking action the night prior when the VC had been setting it. Our talk was therapy for me, and Paul said it had helped him also. After ten months in Veterans Administration (VA) hospitals and five major surgeries, he recovered and married, and now has a daughter and two grandchildren. He told me, "Dave, I probably couldn't win a race, but am grateful for the use of all my limbs."

I told Paul that I had always thought that he was living in a VA facility without legs, similar to Lieutenant Dan (Gary Sinise) in the movie Forrest Gump.[26] We talked, shared stories, and exchanged some pictures. Later, we met in Washington, DC, at a Second Battalion, First Marines Vietnam reunion (the first one for both of us). Paul graciously chauffeured my wife, Connie, and me around the city as we visited the marine base in Quantico, the Marine Corps Museum, and other patriotic historical places. Later, I introduced Paul to James Dew, the corpsman who had saved his legs and arm (and possibly his life) by applying tourniquets and bandages to his limbs immediately after Paul had tripped the booby trap. Doc had used Lieutenant Perra's M16 as a splint to stabilize one of his badly mangled legs. He had Lieutenant Perra on a medevac chopper heading to the Da Nang hospital in less than twenty minutes from the time Paul had tripped the booby trap. Their personal reunion was the first time they had met since the tragic incident forty-six years prior.

During our visit to Quantico, we stopped to pay our respects to Lieutenant Colonel Leftwich at his memorial statue. He had been our battalion commander early in our deployment and had died in a helicopter crash after leaving to become commander of the First Recon Battalion. His chopper had gone down in the Que Son Mountains while he was commanding an emergency extraction of members of one of his recon squads (Lieutenant Colonel Leftwich, who had been on his second tour in Vietnam, had gone on all his men's emergency extractions).

The men and women we met and observed while on base were professional and proud marines. We were witnessing firsthand the Marine Corps—as now advertised, "The Few, the Proud, the Marines." Connie and I were honored to walk among them and to be escorted by Paul, a two-time Purple Heart recipient and an amputee (Paul had lost a finger on his right hand). Times had changed from when "McNamara's morons" infiltrated and diluted the armed forces.

3.5. The Lost Grenade/Fragging

When we moved our position, prior to camping in the cemetery and Lieutenant Perra tripping a booby trap, I lost a grenade. When I had become squad leader, I had been issued eight grenades for the entire squad and had been told that I was to track them daily and replace the ones I used for combat by ordering them from supply on the next chopper. I had thought that this was because a lost grenade might end up in the hands of the enemy. I would learn years later that it was designed to prevent fragging. When on perimeter watch, I would always lay the eight grenades around my foxhole, where I could easily grab them in case we were attacked. The next day, Fitz and I (and sometimes others) would place them on our belts prior to leaving our perimeter. When I discovered that I only had seven grenades, I searched the area, even digging around the foxhole with our e-tool (small shovel). The eighth grenade was never found.

Was the missing grenade intended for someone in our platoon? Fragging was a vigilante way of refusing to obey orders or retaliating against a superior for an unpopular act or order. It was mostly used against officers, but it was also used on NCOs. It was performed by anonymously tossing a live grenade into an officer or NCOs range, normally at night. During just the four years in Vietnam when this was officially tracked (by the army), approximately one thousand cases of fragging occurred, resulting in eighty-six deaths and 714 injuries.[27]

There were rumors that many of the soldiers wanted Staff Sergeant Beck killed because he was a danger to everyone and had already cost lives and casualties during his time assigned to our platoon. There was a bounty on his head to be paid to whoever killed him (the bounty was common knowledge among the grunts in our platoon, some of whom had agreed to pay their share when the act was complete). There were some soldiers who did not like Lieutenant Timberlake, mainly because he prohibited pot smoking and boom-boom girls. Discipline was unpopular in Vietnam, especially with the shit birds. Then there was me, Corporal Gerhardt, who had written up Bean and Roadie for disobeying orders. Sergeant Cracker, a veteran marine on his second tour, told me (after I had written up the two marines in my squad) that it was a dangerous thing to discipline anyone while in Vietnam.

Of course, the mystery of the lost grenade will never be solved. Perhaps I left it behind, and it ended up in VC hands and was the same grenade Lieutenant Perra tripped. Possibly, another marine took it during the night after I had set the grenades out around my foxhole, with the intention of fragging someone in our platoon. If Bean or Roadie did have the missing grenade, saving their lives prior to Lieutenant Perra's tripping the booby trap might have ironically saved mine by giving them second thoughts. There could be other possibilities as to why it disappeared and where it ended up. It is an unknown that has weighed heavily on me for many years as I wish I had not lost track of it and had reported it to authorities immediately upon noticing it was missing. I was never informed that the main reason we kept count of them was because of fragging concerns. I gained this knowledge years later and would have reported it if I had had this information at the time.

Notes: It was difficult to find and prosecute fraggers since it was generally done after dark with no witnesses. Only ten American soldiers were convicted of murder by fragging.[28]

How concerned were officers about being fragged? In the army, Major Colin Powell (a future four-star general) said he was "living in a large tent and I moved my cot every night, partly to thwart Viet Cong informants who might be tracking me, but also because I did not rule out attacks on authority from within…."[29]

3.6. The Rocket Belt

The Rocket Belt (also referred to as the "killing zone") was a large area stretching south and west of Da Nang, where the VC recurrently launched rockets at marine and ARVN positions and the Da Nang airbase. The VC in the area seemed to have an unlimited supply of Russian-made 122mm rockets.

Fast-forward forty-five years: I received an email on August 14, 2016, from Paul Stevens, who had noticed a post I had made on a Marine Corps social network showing that I had been in the same platoon at the same time he was, but he did not recognize me. Here is the initial exchange:

(From Stevens): Dave, I was in 1st Plt Fox from July 70 to June 71. I was CPL Stevens, a squad leader.

Paul Stevens

(From Gerhardt): Hi Paul. I was one of the squad leaders also. It was interesting to see your pictures and that you also went to Iraq.

Note. I remember that skeleton head from op in Laos. Haha
Semper Fi

(From Stevens): Hell yea, I remember you! You had a tough job controlling that squad. How are you? Remember when we set up next to that arvn compound, you had to go out on ambush. The arvns got hit and 122's started firing off all around us. There was movement everywhere and y'all were stuck out there. It was a big firefight right next to us.

Paul

(From Gerhardt): The night you're talking about, I had claymores set and couldn't get to them to disarm and start back. Our gunships wanted to fire but couldn't because I was caught there.

(From Stevens): That was a wild night. We had a major firefight less than 100 meters from our perimeter and rockets launching around us. I'll keep in Touch

Paul was mentioning a night when our platoon was operating in the Rocket Belt and Lieutenant Timberlake commanded me to move my squad to coordinates beside an ARVN compound in a small-forested area. I found a perfect location for an ambush and set us up in a grove of trees overlooking a small but deep ravine. It was a moonless night in an enemy-infested region of the rocket belt, and most of us recognized the danger, including Lieutenant Timberlake—who took the rare move of sending our platoon's entire machine gun squad with me. He also instructed me to set out two claymore mines. I positioned our setting in a straight line overlooking the ravine and separated the two machine gun teams, placing them in the middle of my men on either flank.

The M18 claymore was a lethally-explosive anti-personnel mine, approximately eight by five inches, that exploded when triggered by a small handheld detonator (called a clacker). The claymore and clacker were attached to separate ends of a long wire. The claymore was curved on both ends and blasted seven hundred steel balls (one-eighth of an inch each) one-hundred-plus meters toward the enemy at a sixty-degree-wide arc.[30] It also had a back blast. Therefore, we were not to set them too close to our position, slightly angle their back away from us, and we were to take cover when they were detonated. To be sure we aimed it the correct way, the words "front toward enemy" were printed on one side in large letters. Each claymore came in an individual pack with long straps that could be thrown over our shoulders for carrying. Inside the bag were three separate parts: the mine (with attached folding legs designed so the claymore could be placed almost anywhere and stand on its own), the detonator, and a one-hundred-foot roll of wire attached to a blasting cap that fitted on the claymore itself.

Normally, claymores are set outside a perimeter in the daylight. It was unusual to set them after an ambush was in place, but they could be lifesavers in case of an enemy attack. With both claymore bags strapped over my neck and resting on my back, I cautiously crawled into the ravine, about forty feet from our position, and set up the first claymore by removing it from its bag, unfolding the feet, and placing it at a slight angle to our left facing down the gorge. I next took out the wire and attached the blasting cap to the mine. I then crawled to my right approximately thirty feet, unwinding the wire attached to the first claymore, and repeated the same procedure with the second one, aiming it at a slight angle to the right. I crawled backward up the ravine toward our ambush site, unwinding both wires. Once safely back, I attached the ends of the wires to clackers and placed them both in front of me. If I needed to blast them, I would simply move a safety and squeeze the trigger on each clacker.

We had been out for approximately two hours and were on high alert when enemy rocket fire started blasting an ARVN compound on the edge of the woods that we were in, less than a hundred meters from our ambush site. Enemy rockets were exploding between our platoon perimeter, where Lieutenant Timberlake and the rest of our marine unit were, and us. Small arms fire followed, including enemy AK-47 sounds. I grabbed both clackers and tried to see into the dark for any movement as I readied to set them off. The ravine seemed to be the only safe passageway for the VC once they decided to cease their attack and pull back. Back at our platoon, the radioman had ordered night sunshine, and it dimly lit up the area in front of us, enabling me to at least look for shadows or movement.

Shortly thereafter, a Cobra gunship appeared, buzzing the area including the sky immediately above us. Lieutenant Timberlake came on the radio and ordered me to return to our platoon's perimeter immediately so the gunship could fire into the woods where we were. There were two problems with that order: rockets were still blasting the ground between our platoon and us, making our return unsafe, and I had to retrieve—or blow—the claymores. I decided to retrieve them.

I first disconnected the clappers and alerted the squad not to fire. I crawled toward the first mine, following its wire down the ravine and winding it around my left hand as I went. Next, I found the second one and wound its wire around the same hand as I crawled back. I became disoriented and was not sure if I was heading back in the right direction—until my butt hit the barrel of a machine gun. By now, the lieutenant was screaming at me over the radio to return to his perimeter. The gunship was still circling, but the lieutenant would not allow it to fire until he confirmed that we were safely out of the area. The enemy rockets had stopped, and we quickly hustled back to our platoon. A furious Lieutenant Timberlake met me as we entered the perimeter. For the first time, I had a heated exchange with an officer. He wanted to know what had taken me so long. I fired back that I had a perfect setup, with two machine guns and two claymores that could have annihilated the enemy as they were retreating. The reason it had taken so long was that I had had to retrieve the claymores. He seemed to understand, or at least he didn't push it.

It is no wonder that Paul Stevens remembered this night. The two of us had talked the next day, and he had suggested that I should have just blown the claymores and gotten us out of there. I had considered doing just that and agreed with Stevens that it would have been the safest way to handle it because I would not have needed to crawl outside our perimeter to retrieve them. We could have left immediately, allowing the gunship to blast the area. It worked out, though, since during the time I was retrieving the claymores, the enemy rockets stopped, enabling our safe passage back. Although I agreed that I had made a poor decision, I did not agonize over it—as I would have if we had not all returned safely.

We learned the next day that a squad of VC had attacked and penetrated the ARVN compound, killing five of their soldiers. It had been a mistake to order us out, even in order to enable the gunship to fire. The ravine we were watching was the enemy's only path of escape, and we were waiting in the perfect location for a surprise ambush, with two machine guns, two claymores, twelve riflemen with M16s, and a blooper man—all pointing into the ravine. It would have been great payback for what they did to the ARVNs. I realized that I was lucky the VC had not been there when I crawled into the ravine by myself to retrieve the claymores, or if they were there, they were wise enough not to blow me away—for it would have stirred a hornet's nest.

3.7. Naval Corpsmen and Military Docs

"God created corpsmen so marines could have heroes."

The above quote was once expressed to Ron Bobele (Corpsman "Doc Bo" of Echo Company, 2nd Battalion, 1st Marines, 1969-70) by a fellow marine. As a division of the navy, the marines used the navy corpsmen as their medical colleagues. Fondly called docs, the navy corpsmen were our saviors in Vietnam. Without them, the list of names on the Vietnam Veteran's Memorial in Washington, DC would be much lengthier.

In addition to aiding American soldiers, the US medical teams did a lot of good for the people in Vietnam, treating injuries from bullets and bombs, broken bones, and diseases such as malaria, cholera, and smallpox. The children in outlying villages, who had never received skilled medical attention, were primary recipients. On one occasion, an army doctor, Lawrence H. Climo, rode an elephant four hours (one way) through the jungle to treat people in a village that was otherwise inaccessible.[31]

We were taught early in training to respect Naval Corpsmen. In boot camp for example, our DI told us that as a division of the navy, it was our duty to "take care" of navy wives while the seamen were out to sea. He emphasized that marines were, "the best fighters and the best lovers." He added, "stay away from corpsman wives—her husband may someday have your life in his hands."

Note: A total of 2,086 naval corpsmen and their army medic counterparts are listed on the Vietnam Memorial in Washington, DC. Medics and corpsmen also medically aided the Vietnamese, both friendly and foe. On at least one occasion, a navy corpsman delivered a baby.[32]

Fast-forward forty-six years to when I attended my first reunion of the Vietnam veterans of the Second Battalion, First Marines. In a crowded room were Purple Heart recipients, amputees, officers, and other marines who had been through unimaginable incidents in Vietnam, many now suffering from post-traumatic stress disorder, Agent Orange-caused diseases, and other medical problems associated with their respective time spent serving in Vietnam. However, the most respected men in the room were the docs. These were the guys whom, all those years ago, we could not have done without. As we remembered some of the injuries and medevacs, the question always arose: "What doc did you have?" These wartime first responders administered medical aid amid some of the worst conditions imaginable—under fire, in any terrain, with narrow provisions, and with inadequate time. They carried medical bags but also M16s, taking part in firefights until they were needed to perform medical miracles.

3.8. The Black Clap

Marines learned about the "black clap" early in training from "reliable" sources such as the DIs and in venereal disease classes. There were also Vietnam vets who swore it to be true. The black clap (also known as "Hong Kong dong," the "grand slam," and, in the army, as "black syph") consisted of a resistant venereal disease strand that was not curable with antibiotics and came with excruciating pain, especially when attempting to urinate. We were told that our manhood would turn black and fall off within weeks of contacting it and that there was no cure. The military sent all those infected by the black clap to suffer a horrible death in a clandestine locale in the Pacific that was a former leper colony. At one end of the island was an incinerator where they cremated all corpses to prevent further contamination to creatures of air, land, and sea. Their relatives would be told they were killed in action/body not recovered or missing in action.[33]

As silly as this myth sounds, I believe it was an effective deterrent for some soldiers to keep them away from cathouses and pup tents and encouraged others to use a "raincoat." Venereal disease (primarily syphilis and gonorrhea) was an ongoing problem for military personnel (as it has been in most other wars) and could affect a unit's strength by reducing the number of men left in the field to fight. We were told in stateside classes that a soldier could face a court-martial for having to leave his unit during time of war for venereal-disease treatment. To my knowledge, discipline for contracting venereal disease never happened in Vietnam, although some units frequently sent men to the rear for penicillin shots. Navy corpsmen could request and administer penicillin in the field but were instructed to send venereal disease patients to sickbay in the rear.[34] This meant that the medical diagnosis and related treatment would be permanently recorded in the patient's military medical file. However, certain corpsmen would treat friends, officers, and high-ranking NCOs off the record when requested or when commanded to do so—in order to prevent the Marine Corps from knowing the patient's dirty little secret.

When Lieutenant Timberlake took command of our platoon, the pup tents outside our perimeter disappeared, along with venereal disease cases. He allowed the Coke and beer vendors to continue supplying us.

Note: Congress passed the Privacy Act of 1974 (Public Law 93-579), Authorization for Disclosure of Medical or Dental Information (DD Form 2870).[35] Military members and veterans now have the option of disclosing their medical records to a third party by voluntarily completing and signing this form, but some ex-military politicians have refused to do so. I suspect that one of the reasons for this lack of political transparency is venereal disease treatment (or treatments) in their health records.

3.9. The Arizona Territory

Prior to starting my tour in Vietnam, returning veterans warned us about the Arizonas. One of our instructors, Sergeant Ski (his nickname), a proud Polish instructor, had served two tours of duty in Vietnam and had earned three Purple Hearts. After one of his classes, he stayed around for a "bullshit session" with a few of us who wanted more time with him, answering our questions about Vietnam and the dangers we were going to face. He specifically mentioned an area known as the Arizonas. I found that it was every bit as dangerous as described by Ski and others. The Arizona Territory was an enemy-infested area southwest of Da Nang and in our tactical area of responsibility. Because it stretched to the border with Laos, the enemy was well supplied via their own inlets off the Ho Chi Minh Trail.

The Arizona Territory had it all—VC who set multiple booby traps, well-concealed snipers, night ambush squads, and company-sized units of the North Vietnamese Army capable of a full-frontal attack. We were extra cautious, especially when on patrol. It was common knowledge that the VC marked booby traps so they could find and disarm them later if necessary and to warn locals so they could avoid them when travelling down the paths and dykes. We were wary of any stick or stone that seemed out of place and were taught that three of something (rocks, sticks, etc.) meant a booby trap and that there might also be a marker that pointed toward them, usually a stick. When we had Vietnamese Popular Forces with us, we would give them the honor of walking point, trusting that they knew the markings and areas to avoid, but if they did not—it was their war.

During my first week as squad leader, I replaced our point man with Fig. Specialty classes were set up for troops in Vietnam, including a Vietnamese-language class, map reading, and land mine school (a.k.a. point man school). Fig attended the three-day landmine school, where he became an "expert" on booby traps. During one of our trips to the Arizona Territory, he pointed out a booby trap. It was marked with three small stones pointing in a straight line where the ground had been disturbed and then covered with weeds. It was not very well done, contrary to what we had heard—that the Viet Cong were camouflage experts. We were traveling just off a path where the booby trap appeared to be. A doll was lying a few feet from it.

Ski said the VC knew that Americans liked toys and would use them to lure us into an area where there was a booby trap. He specifically mentioned baby dolls. He also mentioned that they knew we liked collecting souvenirs and not to be tricked into going after their flags, which they would set beside booby traps. Later in training, we were shown a drawing of a Vietnamese flag attached to a bamboo pole. A wire was fished through the interior hollow part of the bamboo, from its top to the ground, where it was attached to a grenade.

The evening prior to Fig spotting the booby trap with the baby doll, we were camped in the chest-high grass that the Arizona Territory was known for. It was an uneventful night but unusual because all three squads stayed in to guard the perimeter. Our company commander, Captain Nesbit, was with us and had intelligence that we needed to stay together in full strength. The following morning, I heard something and then spotted it just ten meters from our foxhole. As daylight replaced darkness, I identified it as an enemy flag on a bamboo pole flapping in the slight breeze. As daylight progressively dawned, we saw flags surrounding our entire perimeter. They were a distinctive bright red with a yellow star in the center and only twelve inches in length.

I can only describe this early morning surprise as eerie. The enemy obviously knew the exact location of our perimeter and had encircled us leaving only ten meters between us. The bright-red flags stood out in the natural-colored habitat of the Arizona Territory like cherries atop a sundae heaped with whip cream. There were approximately twelve flags surrounding us exclaiming, "We know where you are and could have killed you if we wanted to!"

In a much smaller but similar way, I could relate to the feelings of Davy Crockett and Colonel Travis when Santa Anna's army surrounded them at the Alamo. Why didn't our enemy kill all of us? My first thought was that only a few VC had carried it out and they knew better than to engage us in an open firefight. They had most likely booby-trapped some or all of the flags, hoping to take some of us out the cowardly way. There was another possible reason, which we were to uncover the following day. Nonetheless, it served a purpose—the strange feeling of being surrounded by enemy flags scared the shit out of us.

This was the second time I deserved credit for saving Bean's and Roadie's lives. They were sneaking out toward the closest flag when I spotted and ordered them both to return. Bean said he was just getting one as a souvenir. I answered that they were booby-trapped. His reply revealed his impulsive nature. As an obvious acknowledgment that he had also heard that the enemy booby-trapped souvenirs, he answered, "Oh yeah" as they both instantly returned to their foxholes without protest.

We packed up and left in a single file, splitting an area between two flags without incident. Our entire platoon moved less than two klicks (two thousand meters), crossing a paved highway built by the Army Corps of Engineers, and set up our perimeter in more tall grass as we dug the deepest foxholes to date.

A later thought: That first night would have been an ideal situation where the feeler antennas (the ones Sergeant Beck had sent back to the rear) could have notified us of enemy activity outside our perimeter while they were setting bamboo poles with flags.

In the early afternoon of that same day, a chopper came near our position on its way back from supplying another Fox Company platoon camped just a mile south of us. As it passed near the campsite we had occupied the day and night prior, the chopper came under heavy enemy AK-47 fire. The attack came from the treed area that we had camped next to. The chopper continued on as the machine gunner on its port side blasted back at them. Our platoon was due to receive the next supply chopper. Lieutenant Timberlake ordered Stevens's squad and my squad, along with two machine-gun teams, to set up an ambush along our side of the road dividing us from the enemy's location. The road was only five-hundred meters from the tree line where the enemy had originally fired at the aforementioned chopper. We totaled thirty men, with two .60-caliber machine guns and two grenadiers, as we secretly traveled and lined up on the opposite side of the road from the enemy. We were anticipating that they would fire on our supply chopper, just as they had the first one.

Our platoon radioman guided our supply chopper's approach away from the small forest, but it was still necessary to bring it from the same direction since other approaches would bring the chopper over one of the treed areas that surrounded us. It came in without incident, but on its way out, AK-47 gunfire opened up on it from the same line of trees where the other chopper took fire from, even though this chopper was farther away. We had stayed well concealed on the other side of the road, but as the enemy began to fire, we popped up from our positions and fired at the tree line and the flashes from their rifles. The enemy immediately turned their fire toward us. In the beginning, our fire was concentrated at one area on the point of the forest, but the enemy opened up on us from other areas throughout the line of trees (approximately one hundred meters wide). We quickly adjusted and began to distribute fire throughout the tree line. I emptied six magazines of twenty rounds each as I fired my M16 on its semiautomatic setting. As I was firing, I was yelling out for everyone to "aim lower." I was taught in sniper school that in a firefight, everyone tended to aim high while attempting to keep his head down where it was not exposed to the enemy's fire. Additionally, and although there is very little recoil with an M16, it does rise when fired rapidly. Accurate fire superiority wins firefights. In other words, firing too high over the enemy's head is not going to stop them from firing at you. This firefight went on longer than most, but we eventually gained fire superiority, and the AK-47 bullets that were whistling over and around us stopped. Corporal Stevens called to "hold fire." I immediately asked for a body and injury account from all teams, starting with mine. After everyone was reportedly accounted for, I ordered everyone to check his safety and then to pull back—two teams at a time. After a firefight, there is an exploitation phase in which you pursue the enemy and search the area (bodies, prisoners, weapons, and Intel info). In this case, we were ordered by our company commander to return to our platoon's perimeter, and the Fox platoon, whose supply chopper had initially been fired upon, was instructed to search the area up to the edge of the woods. The squad that stayed back to guard our perimeter shared its ammo with members of our two squads that were in the firefight, until we were resupplied the following day.

The chopper safely made it back to our home base. The corpsman on the flight later reported that the machine gunner on the port side was firing his M50 machine gun into the tree line also. The following day, Lieutenant Timberlake informed me that four civilians were hit by our gunfire, but he did not have any additional information about them. I was astounded that there was a village behind the bushes and trees where we had fired. It was obviously well concealed and was the same area and tree line we had camped next to the prior night. We were only a couple hundred meters away from an obviously dangerous VC village that the Arizona Territory was known for, but no people or households had been spotted by anyone in our platoon. It might explain why they did not engage us when they surrounded us with their flags. However, it was stupid of them to snipe at our helicopters from the edge of their village—twice.

The lieutenant said that he believed most of the enemy were killed or wounded. They were not prepared for such a bombardment of gunfire and blooper-launched grenades aimed at them from their flank. Our two-.60-caliber machine guns, along with the .50-caliber on the chopper, were unloading five- to six-hundred rounds per minute each. There were twenty-four of us firing M16s (some on automatic fire at seven-hundred rounds per minute and most on semiautomatic at forty-five to sixty rounds per minute) and two grenadiers releasing multiple M79 grenades. The chopper pilot estimated that there were eight to twelve enemy soldiers who returned fire. However, no kills could be confirmed, and none were recorded.

It is difficult to describe the thoughts and feelings I experienced during a firefight. The enemy was aiming to end my life, as I was theirs. Any one of the hundreds of bullets being exchanged could be lethal. It would have been a bad time to take my blood pressure. My heart was always racing as I realized I was in a real life-threatening event. My heightened senses propelled me into a surreal arena as the gunfight escalated… and then ended as quickly as it began. Once relief washed over me and my heart slowed, I would look around—as my thoughts adjusted to the well-being of my comrades and my responsibilities. It was a horrific event, but amazingly the ultimate rush.

In retrospect, I am amazed at how mechanical we were. As trained, I would empty a twenty-round magazine in the direction of the enemy, partially roll onto my left side while discharging it, grab a loaded magazine off my belt, feed it into the slot in my rifle, release the bolt that inserted the magazine's first round into the chamber (the hammer always remained cocked from the last round of the previous magazine) while rolling back over into the prone position, and continue firing. This sequence took only a few seconds, but it seemed like eternity. Because the entire process became mechanical as trained, there was no conscience interference that might prevent one of the steps of the magazine exchange to be overlooked due to nervy battle intensity, which is always present during frontline combat.

Although the military would tell us that our ultimate goal of a firefight was to kill as many enemies as possible, in reality our intention was to quiet them with overwhelming firepower, and if we killed some, all the better. We just wanted it to be over. In most firefights, we could not see the enemies' faces and were shooting at flashes and sounds from their weapons. This is different from a sniper who carefully takes aim at an unsuspecting enemy combatant. A sniper's goal is his motto:

One Shot, One Kill

Afterward, the squad leader must take charge of organizing his men for additional assault, retreat, and medevacs when necessary. When applicable, he must call for fire (normally mortars from the fire-support base), air support, or illumination (at night), or specify these instructions to the squad's radioman. His responsibilities, training, and experience enable a leader to ignore his own fears and stay "anxiously composed" under fire. One analogy is that the brain goes into a composed mode out of necessity, enabling certain individuals to make decisions and communicate effectively, even under extraordinary circumstances.

Note: Our engagement with the enemy in the Arizonas, with thousands of rounds fired by both sides, was one of the marines' last significant firefights of the Vietnam War. Firefights would become a nominal part of future warfare as improvised explosive devices (a.k.a. roadside bombs), suicide bombers, snipers, and drone and rocket attacks would become our future enemies' preferences.

3.10. A Transformation

As my time in Vietnam passed and as I felt the heartbreak of war, my personality transformed from what was a happy-go-lucky and naïve past to becoming much more serious about our mission in Vietnam. The reality of living in a war zone took a while for me to cultivate, but once it did, I began to rapidly transform into a more serious and confident combatant that was more in tune with our intense surroundings. I wondered how I compared to the many soldiers before me. Innocence does not spontaneously disappear from within once a soldier's boots first tread onto foreign soil, but the graveness of being in a war zone will at some point transform the personality of every warrior. Years after my tour in Vietnam, I compared my photo on my last military ID card to my high school picture, taken just four years prior. The look in my eyes on the ID card speaks the proverbial one thousand words.

My personal and naïve world was always a patriotic one, where my dad and uncles had fought in World War II, and my mom and family loved God and country. It was an awakening to discover that not all marines were as patriotic as I was, and it was even shocking to discover that some did not seem devoted to our mission. About midway through my tour, I became aware that our actions would not have any effect on the war's outcome. I went to Vietnam believing I was going to help my country win a war. Many of my comrades felt the same way. After a while, I started to be influenced in a way that grunts are not supposed to be. In order to be willing to fight and die for their country, warriors must believe they are fighting for a worthy cause. One of my favorite books in high school was a novel about World War I by Erich Maria Remarque, *All Quiet on the Western Front*. [36] Paul Baumer, a German soldier and the main character, wonders why the French and English soldiers are fighting against him on the western front, since Germany is fighting for a righteous cause and the other countries are the evil ones. He then wonders if the French and English soldiers also believe that their respective countries are right and are therefore fighting and willing to die for their homelands the same as he.

Likewise, American soldiers fighting in Vietnam needed to believe in a purpose. Initially, the armed forces did a good job teaching and enforcing the values of loyalty to our country and commitment to our mission in Vietnam. Most of us graduated from boot camp ready to defend our country from communism. However, as the American populace turned toward peace, as the students staged demonstrations on college campuses, as TV news began to use its powerful influence negatively reporting on Vietnam, and when the newspapers and weekly journals regularly criticized our involvement, I began to be influenced the opposite way of what previously had been a powerful commitment to my country's purpose in Vietnam. I began to question my will to risk death for a cause that I was no longer sure about; however, I would have risked my life to protect any one of the members in my squad.

In retrospect, I do not believe that we were a bunch of Paul Baumers fighting for the wrong cause. At the time, communism was believed to be a threat to the free world. It still may be. Nevertheless, we were pawns trapped in a war that we were not going to win—for whatever reasons. It was past time to concede this chess game. We should not enter into wars without an unwavering commitment to win them.

There was not a lot of downtime in the bush. Patrols, perimeter or ambush watch, and sleep were the major occupants of our time. Daily duties including cleansing and shaving, rifle cleaning, and building the day's pup tents. When there was extra time, we would write letters home, read, play cards, talk or hang out in small groups, or play with the kids. In addition, the squad leaders had meetings with the platoon commander or platoon sergeant on the planning of nightly missions. During one of my "think times," I remembered an episode of *Combat!*,[37] in which Sergeant Saunders outsmarted the Nazis, and his squad wiped out one of theirs. One of his men complimented him afterward for leading them to the victory. Saunders reminded him they had lost two good men themselves and if he really was an astute squad leader, they might all be alive. The remembrance of that episode deeply affected me, and I adopted the following approach:

The importance that we all go home trumps
any number of enemies who do not.

Of course, this type of thinking was not in line with the objectives of the Marine Corps, so I kept it to myself. My sole responsibility became to protect all thirteen of us every night and every day when patrolling, setting ambushes, and even sleeping. My goal as a squad leader was to eventually bring us all home safely. It was a lot of stress that I did not recognize at the time, and combined with a lack of sleep, it began to wear on me—that is, until I became accustomed to it and learned to not worry about the individual personalities of my squad or whether I was popular or even liked. This newfound confidence enabled me to better do my job. Lieutenant Timberlake's leadership and backing, support from some members of my squad (especially Fitz), and my restored ability to enjoy humor had positive effects on my leadership abilities. The rest of the squad seemed to trust my decisions and now believed I was not going to get us all shot up, although Bean and Roadie still needed the majority of my babysitting time and were always a safety concern. For example, one day while on patrol, I noticed that Bean was walking with his safety off (it was on the automatic setting). I immediately halted the squad and confronted him, telling him that his M16 could fire at any time and kill one or more of us. Bean always argued everything, including this obviously dangerous misuse of his weapon. He said that we were in an area where we could take fire, and he had to be ready. I told him that the safety was designed to be next to his thumb so he could flick it off while he was raising and aiming his rifle. It would not delay him in firing his weapon at all. He continued to argue while the rest of the squad watched, wondering who was going to win this one. I finally said that he would have to give me his M16 and walk without it if he didn't put the safety on and keep it there. He said a few choice words but put his safety on. Fig and some of the others later agreed with me. Fig said that walking around with your safety off was plain stupidity. I thought it was due to the environment where he was raised. Bean grew up in a large city (New Orleans) and never had the experience of game hunting or even shooting a long gun (a rifle or shotgun). Every hunter knows to always keep his or her safety on until ready to fire. I kept an eye on Bean's safety for the rest of our tour together.

Note: The M16 assault rifle had a thumb latch on the left side above the trigger designed for use by the right thumb when shooting from the right shoulder side. A rifleman had three choices, which were clearly marked as "semi," "safe," or "auto," meaning semi-automatic fire, safety (no fire), or automatic fire. Automatic meant that if you held your finger on the trigger, it would continue to fire until you released it or ran out of ammo from a twenty-round-capacity magazine (approximately three seconds to shoot twenty rounds). Semi-automatic required the rifleman to pull the trigger for every round shot. The safe position was in the middle and facing up, enabling a soldier to easily flick it with his thumb—to the right for semi and to the left for auto.

In some ways, I was able to associate with Bean. We were both youthful rebels fighting a war that permitted too much individualism. I also took liberties that I should not have. For example, I did not wear a helmet or flak jacket most of my time in the bush. I was the only one in a platoon of fifty-plus men who didn't (Fitz called me a "Hollywood marine"). My reasoning was that they were unnecessary weight; plus, the helmet made my head hot and sweaty. I felt that I could think and react better without it. I learned this behavior from watching Smokey Dog, who did not wear a helmet or flak jacket and carried a gangster-era "grease gun." Occasionally, we would receive a command from our headquarters that everyone must wear proper combat gear. During these times I would send a message to the rear to send out my helmet and flak jacket on the next chopper. Shortly thereafter, I would send them back. I look back on this behavior as sheer stupidity and am lucky that my "naked body" was never in the way of shrapnel from a booby trap or speared by punji sticks. Vietnam was a war of rogue independence, where a warrior could carry a gangster gun instead of his issued M16, and helmets and life jackets were noncompulsory.

Note: The flak jacket was a protective vest with body armor and weighed approximately ten pounds. Along with a helmet, it was to be worn mostly for protection from shrapnel and punji-stick-type booby traps. Neither one was capable of foiling a high-powered bullet from piercing our bodies (as from an AK-47 rifle).[38]

A local village girl with her family's water buffalo in a rice paddy

Dave Gerhardt as an awards writer in middle of tour

First swing set for children in a village at the base of the Marble Mountains **Photo: David Hansen**

Buddha Goddess carved inside a Monk sanctuary in a cave in the Marble Mountains

Night "sunshine" with Marines in background

Camping in a village cemetery

Guide dog watching Vietnamese locals outside of marine perimeter Photo: Fred Stalzer

Les Fitzgerald with bamboo viper

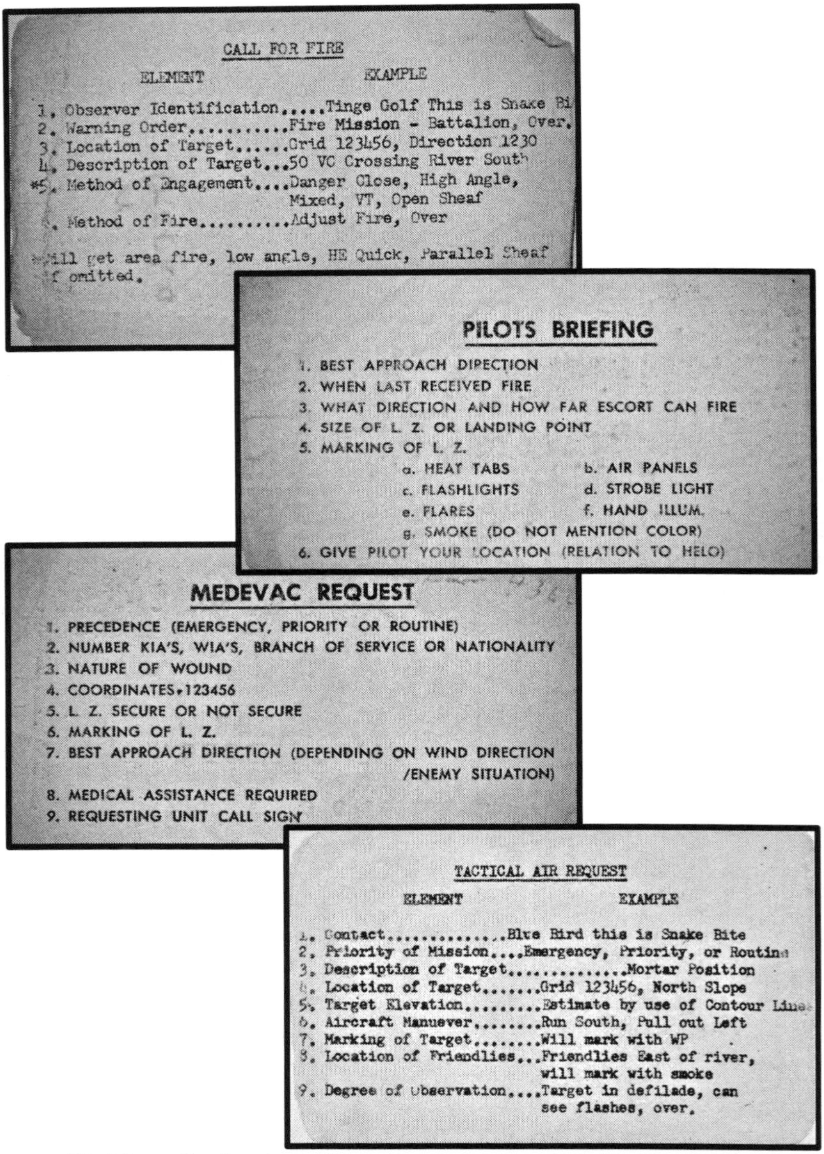

CALL FOR FIRE

ELEMENT — EXAMPLE

1. Observer Identification.....Tinge Golf This is Snake Bi
2. Warning Order..........Fire Mission - Battalion, Over.
3. Location of Target......Grid 123456, Direction 1230
4. Description of Target...50 VC Crossing River South
*5. Method of Engagement....Danger Close, High Angle, Mixed, VT, Open Sheaf
6. Method of Fire..........Adjust Fire, Over

*Will get area fire, low angle, HE Quick, Parallel Sheaf if omitted.

PILOTS BRIEFING

1. BEST APPROACH DIRECTION
2. WHEN LAST RECEIVED FIRE
3. WHAT DIRECTION AND HOW FAR ESCORT CAN FIRE
4. SIZE OF L. Z. OR LANDING POINT
5. MARKING OF L. Z.
   a. HEAT TABS — b. AIR PANELS
   c. FLASHLIGHTS — d. STROBE LIGHT
   e. FLARES — f. HAND ILLUM.
   g. SMOKE (DO NOT MENTION COLOR)
6. GIVE PILOT YOUR LOCATION (RELATION TO HELO)

MEDEVAC REQUEST

1. PRECEDENCE (EMERGENCY, PRIORITY OR ROUTINE)
2. NUMBER KIA'S, WIA'S, BRANCH OF SERVICE OR NATIONALITY
3. NATURE OF WOUND
4. COORDINATES.123456
5. L. Z. SECURE OR NOT SECURE
6. MARKING OF L. Z.
7. BEST APPROACH DIRECTION (DEPENDING ON WIND DIRECTION /ENEMY SITUATION)
8. MEDICAL ASSISTANCE REQUIRED
9. REQUESTING UNIT CALL SIGN

TACTICAL AIR REQUEST

ELEMENT — EXAMPLE

1. Contact..............Blue Bird this is Snake Bite
2. Priority of Mission....Emergency, Priority, or Routine
3. Description of Target.............Mortar Position
4. Location of Target.......Grid 123456, North Slope
5. Target Elevation.........Estimate by use of Contour Line
6. Aircraft Manuever........Run South, Pull out Left
7. Marking of Target........Will mark with WP
8. Location of Friendlies...Friendlies East of river, will mark with smoke
9. Degree of Observation....Target in defilade, can see flashes, over.

Field radio instructional cards carried by Gerhardt

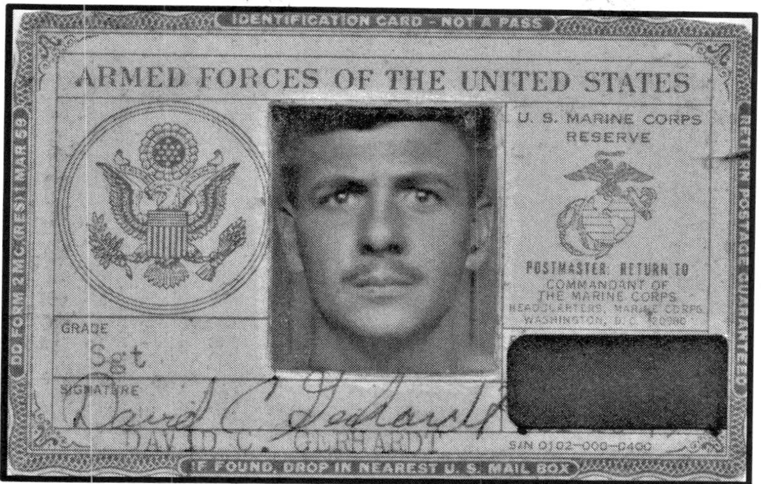

The "Look"
1971 Military I.D. after Vietnam
vs. 1967 High School Photo

James Dew reunites with Paul Perra at 2nd Battalion, 1st Marine Reunion in Washington D.C. 46 years after Doc Dew's actions saved the Lieutenant's legs and arm (and possibly life) in the minutes after tripping a booby-trap
11 November 2017

Dave Gerhardt, Paul Perra, Steve Lepley, and James Dew at the Marine Corps Museum, Quantico, VA. The background picture is a painting set at the Tun Tavern in Philadelphia commemorating the founding of the Marine Corps by the Continental Congress on 10 November 1775
Photo: Consuelo Gerhardt **11 November 2017**

Dave Gerhardt (left) Paul Perra honoring their former Battalion CO, Lt. Colonel William Leftwich, killed in a helicopter crash in 1970

Photo: Consuelo Gerhardt **11 November 2017**

Part IV

★★★

4.1. Salty

Salty is an old navy term referring to sailors who have been at sea too long and thus get slack in their duties. We were warned during training in the States that becoming overconfident could be a dangerous thing to oneself and others. In war, a marine can get salty from being in the bush for a long period of time without enemy engagement. This may lead him or her to believe it's safer than it actually is.

There are times in war that are more life-threatening than others and days and weeks when nothing dangerous happens, but that does not indicate that a soldier is safe from harm. He or she always faces the risk of being killed or injured while in a war zone, especially with an enemy that utilizes guerilla tactics. Guerilla tactics used by the VC included setting mines and hit-and-vanish ambushes while they exploited a massive tunnel system and a portion of the population that sided with them. During my time in the bush, every step could have been a last one. In addition, enemy snipers were an unforeseen threat, day and night. Our snipers had to go on patrol, find camouflaged spots, and quietly await the enemy. The enemy snipers in our area likely resided in local hamlets, and we came to them. When we made camp near their village, they simply sneaked to a favorite nearby location, took a few well-aimed shots at us, and vanished.

A warrior must hold to the fact that the danger level in a war zone is always high. He or she can never let his or her guard down—as I once did. It was late at night toward the end of my tour. Fox Company had not engaged the enemy for a couple weeks and had not found or hit any booby traps. Like normal, I was struggling to stay awake while on night perimeter watch after about twenty-four hours with little rest. Even though I knew better, I stood up and stretched as a means to refresh my tired body and stay awake. Suddenly, two shots whistled by my ear. I recognized the distinct sound of an AK-47 as I instinctively dived into my foxhole and grabbed my M16, aiming it at the area where I had seen two flashes. I flicked off the safety with my thumb to semiautomatic but held fire. I realized that I was aiming at a village where locals were sleeping. I grabbed the radio and reported the sniper. The platoon radioman sarcastically came back with, "Well, fire back at 'em." A marine that was positioned on the other side of our perimeter radioed in to report that two rounds landed in the dirt beside him. I responded to both of them that it was too late to return fire.

The incident would have made a perfect science-class illustration comparing the speed of light to the speed of sound and to that of a bullet. I saw two flashes, heard two shots, and then the rounds whistled within fractions of an inch of my right ear. I can debunk a common belief that you never hear the shot that kills you. I heard the shots prior to the rounds whistling by my head. Had I been hit, I would still have heard the shots, even if they were to be the last sounds I would ever hear.

Throughout the following day and beyond, I had a continuous ringing in my ears, but I realized how fortunate I was. An inch to the right, and my ear would have been taken off. A few inches to the right, and my brains would have been blown out of my head. Also, I could have caused the marine on the other side of the perimeter to be wounded or killed. I realized that it was a stupid and salty thing that I had done. My experience from the firefight in the Arizona Territory, where some of our rounds had hit four villagers, was the reason I withheld my fire on the sniper. It was a similar situation in that the enemy fired upon us from the edge of their village. Trees concealed many villages, making them difficult to discern, especially from a distance, as the area would appear to be an uninhabited forest. The fact that the enemy would start a firefight against us on the perimeter of their village still makes no sense. It is comparable to starting a firefight in your front yard with your family in the house behind you. In this case, I knew of the village and had gained the necessary experience to refrain from an aggressive response.

Note: It is estimated that some two million Vietnamese civilians were killed and many more wounded during the Vietnam War (both North and South).[39]

4.2. Small-Arms Weapons

The Russian-made AK-47 automatic rifle was our biggest small-arms nemesis. It had a distinct "hard" sound when fired, one that American combatants became aware of early on in their deployments. Anyone listening to a firefight between Americans with M16s and VC or NVA fighters with AK-47s would recognize the two sides just by the sounds of the weapons' discharges.

The AK-47 round was larger and a little more powerful than our M16 rounds. It was designed to tear through flesh and bones as it entered one side of the body and exited through the other. The AK-47 was also a better sniper rifle than ours due to its longer range.

The lighter, American-made M16 semiautomatic assault rifle shot a round slightly smaller but could do more internal damage than the Russian-made AK-47. "If you nail a gook with your M16 and two of his buddies have to help him back to their rear, you now have three fewer AK-47s aiming at you," stressed our boot camp DI weapons instructor. He next got a laugh from most of us: "Of course, with his mangled guts hanging outside his stomach, he will meet his maker—it just might take an hour or so."

Our M16 was a superior rifle for jungle warfare and close contact because of the agility it allowed us when maneuvering through difficult terrain, ease of magazine exchange, and the location of the safety.[40] In addition, it had less kick and could therefore be fired from either the shoulder or hip. Our stateside weapons instructor said that the round was designed to enter its target and then turn (cartwheel) as it passed through, thereby causing more destruction to the inside of the human body by ripping through vessels, organs, bones, or anything in its path. If it exited, it would make a larger hole than the one it made upon entry. Some countries had questioned its legality with Geneva Convention rules. Conversely, we were told that Geneva Convention criteria required a bullet to make a clean hole upon entry into a human target but did not specify what type of hole it would produce upon its exit. The M16 round was designed to seriously wound its subjects but not immediately kill them. As our DI explicitly explained, a wounded soldier customarily requires at least two others to aid him, taking more guns off the battlefield.

Chest and stomach wounds, by either weapon, were usually deadly unless immediate medical attention was available. The ultimate conclusion: no one on either side wanted to take a round from an enemy rifle.

4.3. Sandbagging and Faking

Shortly after the night I almost took one in the ear, I was preparing to go on a night-ambush patrol. After I received the coordinates, I followed our route on my map and reviewed it with Fig, who had to know the route in order to walk point. We were to head east for three klicks to checkpoint one, turn right for three klicks to checkpoint two, go straight for four klicks to checkpoint three, and turn left for four klicks to checkpoint four and our final destination.[41] Fig, in his normal canny manner, pointed out that it was risky because we were zigzagging too much in a known booby trap area.

I replied to him to just take us to checkpoint one, and we would likely sandbag there. I waited until after dark and started the squad in the direction opposite our first checkpoint. Once we were safely away from our platoon (about two-hundred meters), Fig changed direction and headed toward checkpoint one. This was normal procedure in order to mislead the enemy as to the direction we were actually heading, as well as prevent them from anticipating our return route.

Sandbagging was a tactic soldiers in the bush knew quite well. Returning veterans had told us about it before we ever set our boots into the perils of a Vietnam rice paddy. Rather than follow the entire route of a mission, marines would go as far as the squad leader thought was safe and set up for the night. I had learned the art of sandbagging from my first squad leader, who did it as often as he thought he could get away with it. I never heard of a squad who didn't sandbag at least some of the time. It was our answer to the lurking risks of detonating a booby trap and being blown away. When I became squad leader, I sandbagged when I thought it was appropriate for safety—probably about a third of the time. Excessive movement in the booby-trapped areas of operation (AOs) that we were assigned to was suicidal. However, it was not always easy to shorten the walking distance of a patrol. Sometimes we had to move farther than desired to find a dry area among flooded paddies or an appropriate spot for an ambush setting. When on river watch, we always went the entire distance to the banks of the river.

On this night, we traveled about three klicks and settled in on a slight rise in a rice paddy that was not flooded. Fitz whispered on the radio receiver, "Fox Oscar;

this is Fox Oscar/Oscar at Charlie Papa Oscar, over" (Fox one platoon this is Fox one platoon/first squad at checkpoint one, over).

The platoon radioman softly replied, "Roger, Fox Oscar/Oscar. Charlie Papa Oscar, out."

Fitz waited fifteen to twenty minutes and whispered in, "Checkpoint two." And after another fifteen to twenty minutes, "Checkpoint three." And finally, after fifteen to twenty minutes, "Checkpoint four."

I had arranged the men in a tight formation on one side of the rise. Fitz and I were in the middle, near the top, with the others spread downhill on either side of us. We were to keep two men awake while everyone else took turns sleeping. However, just an hour into our first watch, Fig heard voices. He crawled over and tapped me, but by then I had heard them too. It sounded as if the enemy was on the other side of the rise and only about fifteen to twenty meters from us. We quietly woke everyone as they passed the tap down both sides of our ambush lines. I took the radio receiver and whispered for permission to throw a grenade in the direction of the voices. As quietly as possible, I explained to our platoon radioman that we had encountered voices in our ambush site but could not spot the enemy yet. This was an unusual spotting, and the radioman had trouble comprehending what I was trying to communicate to him. I had to repeat myself several times and in different ways. While I was awaiting permission to blow the owners of the voices into various configurations, the enemy kept talking—seemingly not even attempting to keep their voices low. It actually sounded as if two men were arguing, but they were speaking Vietnamese, and none of us could interpret even a word. It was obvious that they had stopped on the opposite side of the rise from us and did not know we were only a few meters away. They were going to be easy confirms, and I was both excited and nervous. It seemed to take all night for the platoon radioman to get a reply from the platoon commander (it was actually about five minutes), and I was afraid they were going to discover us and fire first. However, we were not in a free-fire zone, and I needed permission to engage. Eventually, the voices ceased, and shortly thereafter, the permission to throw grenades came over the radio. I immediately pulled the pin of the grenade I already had in my hand and threw it on the other side of the rise where we had heard the voices. It exploded with a loud boom, and we heard shrapnel land around us, but the mound and the fact we were lying flat protected us. I then instructed Wheat, our blooper man, to launch some sunshine over the area where the grenade hit (nearly straight up). As the dark night turned into day from Wheat's sunshine round, I crawled up the rise and looked onto the other side. I had to wait a few minutes for the smoke from the explosion to dissipate. Once the area became clearer, I was not surprised that there were no enemy bodies. Permission to engage had come too late, and the enemy had moved on. We now had no choice but to move our position, which we had exposed with the grenade and sunshine. Fitz reported the negative findings to the platoon radioman as we moved nearer to checkpoint two and settled in for the night.

The following morning, we returned to our platoon and moved out shortly thereafter. We happened to pass by the place where I had thrown the grenade. There was a perfectly barren circle in the rice paddy approximately twenty meters in diameter. The rice stalks had been totally blown away, showing mostly dirt, and there was a small hole full of water in the middle that was approximately three meters in diameter—at the obvious point of the explosion. I also noticed the area where we had set up our ambush sight, just on the other side of a small mound. It was easily identified by the individual damage we had done to the rice stalks, and it reminded me of deer beds back home. Our platoon—approximately fifty of us—safely continued on, trampling down more rice stalks as we avoided the potentially booby-trapped paths and dykes. The guys in my squad knew what the barren circle was, but we kept it to ourselves. After all, we were not supposed to be there at that time. Fortunately, the platoon commander and the platoon sergeant did not pay the barren space any attention.

There is always a risk of unintended consequences with every deviation from orders. The high command that devises each mission also creates a plan for the entire night's movements in each tactical area of responsibility (TAOR). This nightly plan is coordinated with Vietnamese Popular Force and Regional Force patrols that also circuited our TAOR. The squad leaders who carried out their respective orders were not privileged to information regarding non-American troop movements. After thoughtful analysis of this incident over the years, I have concluded that the soldiers on the other side of the rise were not the enemy at all. The enemy did not talk on patrols. They were not that reckless, but the PFs and RFs might have been. I now believe that the reason for our near encounter with unidentified soldiers was that we were camped out of position and in the path of a later patrol of PFs or RFs. It is like an airplane crashing into another plane that was scheduled to have crossed its path an hour prior to when it actually did. We were fortunate that it took so long to get permission to engage and that my sandbagging did not result in a firefight with friendly Vietnamese forces.

I believe that sandbagging in Vietnam did save lives. It was the grunt's defense against a higher command that did not seem too concerned about how many of our limbs were strewn throughout the Vietnam countryside or the number of us that went home in body bags. These military planners incredulously continued their plan to fight an enemy who, unlike us, had learned from their past mistakes and became militarily smarter. Our enemy had many advantages, such as their indigenous knowledge of the environment, an extensive underground-tunnel system, and support from many of the locals we were trying to help. There is an additional one that has never been recognized by our military or the historians of this war (to my knowledge). The VC simply cared more about their own than our leaders cared about us, especially toward the end of the war. Their nightly missions were designed to keep them out of personal danger and inflict the greatest harm to us. Their creativity in accomplishing this became known as "guerilla tactics." Our enemy's ambushes were intended to "engage and vanish" before we could retaliate. In comparison, our high command ordered dozens of squads, consisting of hundreds of soldiers, to wander around extremely booby-trapped and risky bushwhack areas on a nightly basis, years after it should have been apparent that this was not the way to confront the enemy and win. Our nightly orders were to travel to a chosen area, via a designated route, and set up an ambush. These orders never included any intelligence information concerning previous enemy encounters or booby traps en route to or at our destination. Although I was not privy to high-command decisions, I was never involved in or heard testimony regarding any innovative or useful ground strategy to counter the enemy's guerilla tactics during my tour. We never deviated from our original strategies even though the number of maimed and dead soldiers kept rising. We kept repeating the same maneuvers that had resulted in prior brothers getting ambushed, sniped at, and tripping booby traps. I believe that we were considered a replaceable commodity. This was why soldiers sandbagged. Every extra step we took could be the one to send us home in a zippered bag, or with missing or useless body parts. Killing gooks ultimately became an adverse objective as we struggled to stay alive and shelter each other. As a squad leader, my first responsibility was to bring us all home. Just as the VC did, we were caring about our own.

It was not always sandbagging that caused friendly conflicts. Here is an excerpt from my first book, *Communication Talks, B/S Walks* (titled "Locked and Loaded"):

On a starry moonless night in March 1971, I was one of thirteen US Marines ably positioned in an extraordinary place. We were quietly lying in a parched area of a rice paddy in the then Republic of South Vietnam. I was the squad leader for Fox Company, Second Battalion, 1st Marines, and 1st Squad. Our mission was to set up for a potential night ambush overlooking a dyke used by enemy forces when travelling through the rice paddy. During these missions, we were always in communication with our company command post—via a field radio carried by our squad radioman.

In addition to our squad, Fox had two other squads on patrol or ambush watch in our area of operation. Suddenly, a Marine from Fox Company's 2nd Squad came on the radio frantically saying that there were enemy forces walking through their ambush site and that they were going to open fire upon them. Immediately, another voice yelled into the radio to hold fire—that it was Marines from our 3rd Squad. As it turned out, Fox Company's 3rd squad was on a night patrol and had wandered off course and into the 2nd Squad's ambush site. Their radioman heard the live transmission and was able to react just in time.[42]

Although it never transpired in our platoon during my second assignment in the bush, firefights among friendlies were always possible, and some marines claimed it happened frequently during their tour. We were young men with loaded weapons, apprehensively wandering in the dark.

Sandbagging was not the only way that soldiers faked something while on patrol or an ambush. One of the three rifle squads in our platoon was commanded by Sergeant Cracker (not his real name) and was known as the party squad. They liked their beer and could drink a lot of it. Scheduled to go on ambush patrol one evening, they had members who were "over the limit." Sergeant Cracker decided, on his own, that he would delegate the ambush patrol to a corporal in his squad. He told me later that he was tired and needed some sleep and was fortunate enough to have Corporal Gaines (not his real name) in his squad, whom he could delegate authority to. Although Sergeant Cracker had this right, he had failed to inform the lieutenant and platoon sergeant of his decision. Prior to leaving, Corporal Gaines, who had also put down a few, told me that they had too much ammo and they were going to fake a firefight to get rid of it because it was getting too heavy to hump. It was only about an hour after they left that they pounded the quiet night with rapid fire from their M16s and grenade launcher. It lasted five minutes (way too long for a typical firefight). Fig, always ready to join a good fight, hurried over and asked me if we should get ready to go out in case they needed support. I just smiled and said that I didn't think so. Captain Nesbitt, who was camped with us that night, told our company radioman not to report it because he had seen the squad drinking and did not believe there was ever any enemy. There was a lot of M16 fire but no AK-47 sounds. The following day, Corporal Gaines tried to convince me that even though he had said they were going to fake it, they had really had a firefight with the VC and that the captain should have reported it as an encounter with the enemy. I went along with him and agreed, but added sarcastically, "It sounded like World War III out there." He got pissed and left.

Ironically, a few night patrols later, Cracker's squad (still commanded by Corporal Gaines) actually did encounter VC, face-to-face, and neither side fired a shot. I first heard it on the radio when the corporal called it in a few minutes afterward. Later, he said that the VC came walking right into the squad's ambush site, but he did not know if they needed permission to fire. Both sides were so startled that no one knew what to do. Most of the men in the corporal's squad slept right through it. One of their guys told me that he had found himself staring at a gook just five feet from him. I could tell he was still rattled by the encounter. He was close enough to distinguish that the VC was just a young teenager. He should have blown the youngster away, but he seemed glad he didn't.

The VC could appear and vanish in a flash. Identifying them as hostile and then reacting had to be simultaneous and immediate. The only way to react quickly was through experience, which was something the temporary squad leader lacked. By now, most of us knew that anyone walking through our ambush site was fair game, especially little people wearing black pajamas. The following day, our lieutenant and platoon sergeant were furious. This should have been a confirmed kill or kills—feathers in their helmets. They called the squad leaders to the platoon center and reamed us for not going out on our own ambush patrols. I later told Lieutenant Timberlake that I always went out with my squad. He acknowledged that this was true about Corporal Stevens and me. After these incidents, Sergeant Cracker did also.

4.4 Ham and Eggs in a Can

The person who created ham and eggs in a can should have been forced to eat a can for breakfast every day for a solid year. It was by far the worst selection in the C-rat case ("rats" was short for rations). We had to be drop-dead starving to even open a can of ham and eggs, where we would find this lump of green gunk. There was nothing that could be mixed with it to make it edible. I kept mine in storage in my rucksack for a starvation emergency. I once traded three cans to the village children in exchange for showing me the location of some potential booby traps. They guided me into a small forest where there were two American M79 explosive grenades hidden under some brush. Since we were in the same TAOR, one of these grenades could have been the one that I had skipped across the river when I was a grenadier early in my deployment. Blooper grenades had to be detonated by hitting their tips on surfaces, but they would sometimes land on their sides or even upside down and never detonate. This was especially true if they traveled through some brush at the end of their flights. I gladly tendered my ham and eggs in a can, along with an unopened box or two of C rations, for the two grenades. To this day, it remains the best deal I ever made. As an aside, beans and weenies were boo-coo number one.

In boot camp, we had a class on what to write (or not write) home. The example used by our instructor was a letter that worked itself all the way to a US congressman and the commandant of the Marine Corps. A marine in Vietnam wrote home that his unit had been in the bush for a while and all they had to eat were long rats. Long rats were a type of field rations used when we were not going to be resupplied for a while. They were dehydrated food packages and therefore much lighter and less bulky, enabling us to carry more of them in our packs. They required that we mix them in a cup with water from our canteen, heat them over a small fire using our packaged heat tabs or a chunk of C-4 explosive, and it was chow time! I preferred them to C rats in cans. However, the marine got into trouble for not clarifying to his mother that they were rations. His congressman demanded to know why our soldiers were eating rats. This was a political high point for him: "We send our boys over there and can't even supply them with food, so they have to eat rats."

Our instructor stressed that there were two lessons here: (1) do not use abbreviations and slang when writing home, and (2) do not cry to Mommy. We were encouraged to write home often, to keep it positive, and not to add to our parent's worries. He explained that the number-one complaint the Marine Corps received was from parents of soldiers in Vietnam wanting to know if their sons were alive because they had not answered their letters for a while.

One of the official documents we signed at our last stateside staging point asked, "If you receive a non-life-threatening wound, do you want your designated loved one notified?" I checked no.

There was a joker at the end of the staging tables: "If you die in Vietnam, what color body bag do you want to be brought home in—red, white, or blue?" I went along with it and picked blue as he pretended to write it down.

4.5 Snakes, Mosquitoes, and Centipedes

I once told Fitz that there were two types of mosquitoes—biters and buzzers. Naturally, we both chuckled at this thought. There were mosquitoes buzzing around my face and ears that seemed to never land and there were those that sneaked in low, drew blood, and left in a hurry. The little vampires seemed to never be satisfied, especially as darkness fell and the temperature cooled. Their insatiable appetites may be why they splattered so much blood when whacked. Altogether, they probably carried more human blood than the Red Cross. I took my malaria tablet in timely fashion and kept mosquito spray in my rucksack to use every night, but there was no perfect defense against their onslaught. Mosquitoes were fierce in their search of our blood, penetrating clothing and skin to suck it out of a vein anywhere on our body. They were a part of our daily subsistence in Southeast Asian rice paddies and rain forests.

Notes: It was years later that I was reading an article on mosquitoes and discovered that only the females bite. The fact I discovered on my own that only half of them bite attests to the extent of my exposure in their environment.

There were two types of malaria found in Vietnam (out of four total). We were taught the dangers of contracting malaria and the potential consequences of just one malaria-carrying mosquito bite if we did not take our weekly pills. These included fever, chills, lost consciousness, brain damage, and death.[43]

The infestation of malaria-carrying mosquitoes was just one of our additional concerns in Vietnam. There were also snakes and other creepy-crawlies, the most prevalent of which was the bamboo viper, a small green snake approximately two feet in length. It is a highly venomous snake with long, intimidating fangs, and it was scarcely noticeable in the bamboo trees and jungle foliage that it camouflaged with. We were warned in training that their bites were deadly. Some called them "one-cigarette snakes," implying that if bit, you only had time for one cigarette before death. They were also referred to as "two-step snakes," implying you would die after two steps (one instructor joked that, if bit, you should only take one step). These stories turned out to be classic marine bullshit (I'm fairly sure we could have taken more than two steps), but it alerted us to the danger of these venomous serpents.

When camped in the rice paddies, we would cut down small pieces of bamboo from nearby tree lines to build tents as protection from the heat. We would always whack a bamboo tree several times with our M16 or a stick, which caused the snakes, camped in the tree, to leap to the ground where we could knife or shoot them. However, they frequently slithered safely away. Fitz earned the involuntary title as the Fox Company snake guy when he returned from a "bamboo tent-stake hunt" holding the tail of a headless bamboo viper, which he had decapitated with his Ka-Bar. On another occasion, he was asleep in the jungle when one crawled onto his chest and slept there. Mex was on watch during the early-morning daylight and sprayed the viper with mosquito spray, causing it to crawl off him. Fitz awoke to the sound of Mex killing the snake with the butt of his rifle just a few inches from him.

There did not seem to be that many snakes in South Vietnam when I first arrived. Then, in October 1970—led by super typhoon Joan and a week later Typhoon Kate—the worst monsoon season in nearly a decade hit the northern provinces, including the marines' areas of operation. As the rains flooded most of the lowlands, the troops moved to higher ground, as did the snakes. Correction: Now there were a lot of snakes in South Vietnam. One platoon told me that they set up a day watch around their perimeter and shot at them with M16s as they approached. They claimed that a swimming snake was a tough target, even with a semi-automatic weapon spilling twenty rounds from a few meters away. The marines were eventually moved to the rear, where we aided the Vietnamese people. The typhoons caused flooding problems throughout the marine's TAOR. We unofficially stopped the war to aid the populaces with food, medical care, and temporary shelter, and our helicopter crews went on missions to evacuate stranded civilians.

Note: There are thirty-seven very venomous snakes found in Vietnam, including various types of vipers, coral snakes, and cobras (spitting cobras, jungle cobras, and king cobras).[44]

In hindsight, the flooding caused by the two typhoons would have been an opportune time to check for identification papers while aiding the local people, since their tunnels and underground sanctuaries had to have been flooded.

Fitz was medevaced twice during his tour. The first time was when he took shrapnel from an enemy grenade. He recovered rapidly and returned to his unit in just seven days. His second unscheduled chopper ride was more serious.

While sleeping, Fitz was awakened by a sharp, intense pain radiating from his left knee. He assumed that he had been bitten by some type of insect, but had not seen it. Over the next two days, his left leg swelled to twice its size, the pain tortuous and unyielding. He was finally medevaced to the rear and hurriedly flown to the American military hospital in Guam. The doctor said he was close to losing his leg and was worried that gangrene might have set in. The color of the skin on his left leg, from the lower thigh to his ankle, was turning black. Fortunately, the doctor was familiar with the symptoms, thus enabling him to treat it. He said it was probably the bite of a poisonous centipede, judging from the fang marks. Fitz returned to Vietnam and to his unit three weeks later.

Centipedes were aggressive, life-threatening, poisonous inhabitants, along with numerous species of snakes and spiders. We were unwelcome visitors sharing their small homesteads, twenty-four hours a day, as we camped and slept side by side or on top of them. One bite from any one of millions of these poisonous creatures could be as dangerous as an enemy bullet. The fact that a poisonous arthropod crawled inside his khakis and bit Fitz, causing him to be away from his unit three times longer than his shrapnel wound, underscores the dangers of the creepy-crawly-laden environment of Southeast Asia.

Note: Vietnamese centipedes were common in the rain forests and were an aggressive species with a nasty bite.[45]

4.6. Foxholes

We dug foxholes around our perimeter every evening—each one large enough for two of us. Fitz and I were always together so I could have instant access to his radio. Each squad carried two or three small folding shovels (called "e-tools"), which we shared. The marines who humped shovels were usually those who had the least amount of other gear or weight. Some guys wanted to carry one because they claimed it was extra protection from shrapnel. We would generally sleep beside our foxholes and stand guard in them while awake. The size of foxholes was up to individuals, but our perceived danger level would often determine their depth. When in the rocket belt, we dug a foxhole three to four feet deep. In safer locations, the foxhole might be twelve inches or less. I remember telling Bean that he was not welcome in our foxhole. His foxholes normally looked as if he had barely scratched the earth, and I anticipated him jumping into ours if we took incoming rockets, launched grenades, or enemy fire. Digging a hole in the heat and humidity of

Vietnam was not enjoyable, but war is not a place to skimp on safety. Before we moved on, marines would always restore the land. However, kids would come later and dig them all up again, looking for unopened C-rat cans or anything we might have left behind. We referred to these kids as "grave robbers." They would leave the empty "graves" uncovered and the area looking like a small strip-mining site.

One lazy afternoon while we were sitting or lying on the ground inside our perimeter, we took sniper fire from a tree line approximately eighty meters away. Fitz and I both lunged toward our foxhole to grab our rifles and return fire. I was slightly ahead of Fitz as I reached for my M16, endeavoring to aim it toward the area from which we were receiving fire. My right arm was above the hole and the rest of my body inside in an awkward position as the tall, muscular Irishman hurdled into the foxhole. He partially landed on top of my right shoulder, and I felt a painful pop. Fitz called for the corpsman and Doc Dew crawled (under fire) to our position. My shoulder was dislocated and painful. Doc sat down facing me in the foxhole, placed his boot in my armpit, and pulled my arm toward him by holding my right hand and wrist, instantly snapping it back into socket and relieving the pain.

Meanwhile, our platoon commander organized a squad to move toward the section of the tree line where the sniper was believed to be. This was a common procedure but one I had always distrusted. The VC knew our tactics and used them to bait us. They would snipe at us with the expectation of hitting one or more marines and to lure additional marines toward their now-abandoned position, which they often booby-trapped prior to leaving. As our designated squad left the perimeter, we heard an explosion. Upon entering the tree line, they found a dead VC partially blown away. The VC had not only been a poor shot but had been totally inept at setting booby traps, tripping his own as he was attempting his escape. The squad leader reported to Lieutenant Timberlake on the radio, "We have Oscar Victor Charlie Kilo India Alpha" (one VC killed in action). Lieutenant Timberlake told the squad leader to back out of the tree line and return his squad to our perimeter without getting any closer. Most platoon commanders and higher would have instructed their men to search the body and get his rifle and ammo. However, Lieutenant Timberlake understood the possibility of tripping more booby traps. It was common for the enemy to set two or more mines in the same area, or even a chain of them (called a "daisy chain").

The dead gook, who had been trying to kill and disfigure as many of us as he could and then sneak away so he could someday repeat it, became one of our platoon's last confirmed kills.

4.7. An Eventful, Memorable Night

One of the most interesting and bizarre nights of my tour of duty in Vietnam took place in April 1971. My orders were to take my squad on a patrol toward the Han River where I was to set up an ambush sight. Our mission was to watch for enemy movement.

After dark and just prior to leaving, our platoon received additional orders to find and stop the launch of enemy rockets. Intel, per coded messaging over the radio, reported that the enemy planned to launch Soviet-made 122mm rockets in our TAOR sometime during the night. A new mission was added in front of our river-watch one. I was to take my squad toward a small group of trees on the outskirts of a village where Lieutenant Timberlake had spotted a glimmer of light. Outside lights were not allowed throughout South Vietnam after dark, but villagers often disobeyed this rule, mostly by keeping small campfires. Marines seldom disturbed the people in their villages. This was the first time anyone in our platoon was sent to investigate a night-light near a village, but the lieutenant suspected it was the VC preparing their rocket launch.

The tree line was approximately one mile away, and I instructed Fig to head straight to it. I stopped our movement fifty meters short of our target and gave orders for everyone else to stay quiet and in place while Fitz and I crawled on all fours toward the light. I suspected that an enemy launch site would be guarded and knew that we would not be able to get close with too many men. Even though I was concerned that the two of us could be spotted, I realized that we had a better chance of surprising the enemy if we did not advance with the whole squad. I also knew that if the VC spotted us first, we would most likely be killed or wounded. Fitz and I crawled slowly, quietly, and as low as we could—just as we had done in stateside exercises—with our M16 rifles cradled in our arms while we inched forward on our knees and elbows. Most of our route was through the near-barren land of a harvested rice paddy, but we entered into taller weeds as we neared the village. We stopped and looked up when we heard voices and found ourselves just ten meters shy of a campfire. I had made the mistake of not pausing enough to glance ahead to check our location, especially as we had gotten closer. We were much nearer the light than I had intended. I grabbed a grenade from my belt and quietly observed the situation. Two elderly men were sitting around a small campfire, talking in their native tongue, without a clue that we were only ten meters from them. I put the grenade back on my belt as we quietly began our surveillance. I was deciding on how to react to the situation when the lieutenant came over the radio wanting to know our status. The two men heard the transmission and quickly vanished into their village. Hearing strange voices that close to them at night had to have really startled them. Fitz and I extinguished their fire by kicking a couple of logs and headed back toward our squad's position, as I briefed the lieutenant. Since we only had one radio, and it traveled with Fitz, we stopped short of the squad and then continued slowly as I softly called out to the other members of my squad not to fire—until one of them acknowledged. Once united, our full squad of thirteen men moved toward the river as I refocused on our original mission.

I found a fairly well-concealed site along a high part of the riverbank with foot-high grass. We set up in a straight-line ambush overlooking the river. A decrescent moon scattered glimmering reflections across the water.

We had been on a lot of night ambushes, but there was never one that I could designate as routine. Quietly moving through the night to find a hidden spot with the purpose of engaging a formidable foe in a deadly firefight created tense moments. We had been in the country long enough to see comrades get seriously wounded or killed by booby traps or enemy bullets. Once we settled into our ambush sight, night watch duty created additional challenges. Focusing on the same spot in near-darkness for prolonged periods of time could play tricks on your mind, making it seem like the spot was moving. I tried to move my eyes to different areas in order to prevent this optical illusion, but if I perceived movement, my eyes fixated on just that area. Nighttime river watch could create additional anxieties, especially when we were without ample moonlight. The undulating current, along with traveling debris, could cause suspicion of enemy movement. The current, when moving past still objects such as large rocks or a reef, made it seem like these objects were shifting. The enemy was extremely good at moving personnel and supplies down the river undetected, so any type of movement, real or perceived, had to be taken seriously.

On this night, Fig crawled over and whispered that he had just spotted a submarine. As I said, any movement had to be taken seriously—except sub sightings in a river. I tried to disregard his sighting, but he insisted that he had really seen a sub. I told him to forget it; that it was just a rubber ducky. The tension instantly filled the air as I realized that I had made a big mistake in the way I had dismissed his concern. Fig became irate and loud, allowing his indignation to overtake his sense of caution and professionalism. Although I was speaking softly, we were engaged in a heated argument during a night ambush. He eventually went back to his position, still very pissed at me, and he remained that way for several days.

Notes: The enemy used various river craft to navigate the many inland waterways. Fig later claimed that he was taught in mine school that the enemy used submarines. I have not been able to find evidence that the VC had small, factory-made submersible watercraft that could go inland. However, I do not doubt their ability to devise an underwater boat that would enable them to somewhat conceal their movements. I made a mistake in not trusting Fig's sighting and blowing the crawdads out of that part of the river.

I had a learned distrust for sub-sightings. In high school, guys would try to take their dates to a local dam to park and watch the submarine races. On Saturday night there would be a dozen parked cars on the bank "watching" the submarine races.

Later that night, four 122mm Russian-made rockets were launched just five-hundred meters from us, near the village that Fitz and I had crawled into a few hours earlier. I followed the rockets from the initial launch; watching the fire and smoke as they loudly whistled through the sky and exploded on the ground. One hit a jet-fuel storage tank at the Da Nang air base. The gray-and-black smoke and the acrid smell from the burning fuel filled the night sky, and continued well into the following afternoon.

In the meantime, Corporal Stevens—who, together with his squad, was at his own ambush site, pulled an azimuth from his pocket and shot at the location of the launch site. We had been taught how to shoot an azimuth in Infantry Training Regiment, but very few people grasped it. Corporal Stevens was the only marine I knew who actually used one in Vietnam. It is a compass-type pocket device that can accurately determine an unknown position by shooting the distance of two known locations and then using a theorem and a map to locate the position in question. Stevens impressively located the launch coordinates and radioed in the location to the Fox Company radioman. The company radioman confirmed the transmission, and a short time later, I heard our company commander intervene on the radio: “This is Fox Six. If that last number was just a half-klick east, it would be in the ROK AO, over.”

“Yes, sir. That’s where it actually is,” said Stevens to his commander.

I remember thinking how shrewd that was. Captain Nesbitt “officially” changed the location of the launch site of the VC rockets five hundred meters and into the Republic of Korean (ROK) area of operations—that was adjacent to our TAOR. Hence, as history will show, the ROK forces were responsible for the rockets that hit the Da Nang air base that night, including a jet-fuel tank.

Our squad maintained its location on the banks of the river. During the last few hours of the night, I remained in a prone position, still looking for signs of submarines in a river. The hours of heightened threat were normally from 2100 to 0200, but I remained attentive throughout the remainder of the night. We returned to our platoon early the next morning.

The events of this night are forever impressed on my memory: Fitz and I creeping into a Vietnamese village on all fours, Fig spotting a submarine in a river, a rocket attack just five-hundred meters from our position, the subsequent explosion of a jet-fuel tank at the Da Nang Airbase, and the related politics that played out on the radio.

A retrospective look at this eventful night: the Russian-made 122mm rockets were likely shipped to the VC via the Ho Chi Minh Trail and ultimately down one of the rivers at night (perhaps in a submersible water craft).

Note: Our Korean colleagues were known as the war's badasses. They seemed to value other people's lives a lot less than we did and were not overly concerned about the political rules of war and the humanitarian treatment of prisoners as dictated by the Geneva Convention. There was a rumor that when the Americans could not persuade a prisoner to talk, we would "loan" him to the ROKs. I heard tell that we once captured two North Vietnamese Army officers and needed information from them, but they were hardcore patriots who would not give us information we needed through the interrogation methods mandated by the Geneva Convention, so we sent them to the ROKs' camp. The ROKs took the two prisoners up in a helicopter and asked the lesser officer a question. When he refused to answer, they kicked him out. Next, they turned to the other officer, who immediately started to sing, giving up troop movements, troop numbers, and his wife's breast measurements. Even though there may be a lot of embellishment in this story, it does portray the ROKs' attitude toward war and prisoners. They fought to win.

Part V

★★★

5.1. Operation Scott Orchard

As grunts in Vietnam, we never knew where we might find ourselves. Others made the troop-movement decisions, and we carried them out. In the space of several weeks, we could be camped in a rice paddy, the Rock Pile, the tall grass of the Arizonas, a mountaintop, or a jungle.

A few days after the rocket attack on the Da Nang air base, we were sent to the rear to get ready for a mission that was rumored to be the most significant and dangerous of our tour. During the afternoon, Sergeant Cracker, Corporal Stevens, and I met with our platoon commander, Lieutenant Timberlake. He had just returned from a briefing with the battalion commander. In attendance were the company commanders of Echo, Fox, Hotel, and Golf Companies, and their respective platoon commanders.

In a short standing meeting, Lieutenant Timberlake stated the following: "Tomorrow morning we are going on a mission into the jungle northeast of here to try to rescue American prisoners from an NVA base camp. We will be outnumbered at least three-to-one. This is real—I doubt that half of us will be alive at this time tomorrow."

I remember exchanging shocked glances with Stevens, who reacted with a nervous half smile. The lieutenant explained that this was a secret mission near the neighboring country of Laos. It was believed that some of our POWs were being held in a secluded enemy base camp near the DMZ off the Ho Chi Minh Trail. The NVA, in addition to their superior strength, would be well fortified and had the advantage of familiarity with this region. We were to tell no one the nature of our mission, and to give our men orders to be ready to move out at 0500 the following morning. We were to double all ammo, including M16 magazines, machine gun rounds, grenades, and flares. There was to be no resupply of rations, so we were to take long rats in order to carry enough food for at least seven days. The Lieutenant added a peculiar directive: "And no cameras will be allowed." I assumed that this was a serious mission, and cameras would be a distraction—in addition to taking space and weight better served by a magazine of ammo. I later discovered that the real reason for the camera ban was that we were actually going into the neighboring country of Laos, not near it. The US Congress had enacted legislation that was intended to keep the war from spreading into the neighboring countries of Laos and Cambodia. To that end, we were banned from ground operations in Laos. The brass did not want any pictures that could be traced to a location outside Vietnam. I later discovered that everyone did not obey this order. Cameras in Vietnam were very personal possessions, and trying to disallow them was similar to taking a mother's baby from her.

Note: Marine Corps archives state that Operation Scott Orchard was within the boundaries of Vietnam. My map showed otherwise. We travelled on the Ho Chi Minh Trail that ran only through Laos at the northern location where we were. Although there were inroads off the Ho Chi Minh Trail into Vietnam, these were farther south. The NVA made base camps on the Laotian side of the border where they were politically protected by the US government. The landscape was mountainous and dense with rain forests on both sides of the border of Laos and Vietnam.

Our battalion, consisting of four rifle companies, was to participate in this mission. Each company commander was ordered to draw a straw by the battalion commander and the one who picked the short straw was to be the company to drop into the enemy's base camp (by choppers) and rescue the POWs. The other three companies were to land nearby and battle their ways toward the base site in support of the "short-straw company."

Note: The Echo Company commander drew the short straw, but they missed the enemy camp because their choppers landed at the wrong coordinates.

I do not remember much about the eve of our mission that was to take us deep behind enemy lines. I cannot say what goes through soldiers' minds the night before a large battle knowing that the odds are good that he will die. Some of the guys wrote home. I attempted to put the following day out of my mind and get some sleep, but I was only moderately successful. My biggest concern was that we were the last combat marines in Vietnam. We had no backup and were dropping in to fight an enemy—in their own territory—that outnumbered us by at least three-to-one. We had been taught in our stateside history classes how marines of the past had proudly fought and won while on their own, sometimes against overwhelming odds. Instructors specifically mentioned World War II battles at Iwo Jima and Okinawa and earlier Vietnam battles at Hue and Khe Sanh, where marines victoriously fought the enemy while being greatly outnumbered and taking heavy casualties. One instructor stated that the marines had never called the army for help, but we had bailed out their troops over and over again.

The following are the ending lyrics in "The Marine Corps Hymn":[46]

If the Army and the Navy
Ever look on Heaven's scenes,
They will find the streets are guarded
By United States Marines.

I worried that a general in Vietnam was not going to be the first marine commander to beg the army for help even though we had no other backup in Vietnam. We were going to be on our own.

Note: The idea that the Army had never aided the Marines was mere hyperbole by our instructors. History shows that all branches of our military have come to the aid of one another during war. Whether our commanders would have asked the Army for help on this mission will never be known.

"It's a great day to die in a jungle," Corporal Stevens said as we passed each other the following morning. Perhaps it was, or maybe it was a dreary, rainy day—I don't recall. The marines and corpsmen from Echo, Fox, Gulf, and Hotel companies—more than two-hundred strong—assembled the following morning. We boarded our respective choppers for a ninety-minute flight towards one of our enemy's strongholds.

My thoughts were now fully on our mission and particularly on our final approach and the disembarking process. Would we take fire trying to land or while exiting the chopper? From the gunner's openings, I could see two AH-1 Cobra attack helicopters escorting our transport choppers. [47] Having previously witnessed the Cobra's firepower (into the South China Sea), I felt more secure while in the air. Each of the four companies required nine transport helicopters. At some point, the choppers split as they headed for four separate landing sites. As we dropped towards our landing coordinates, I could see only a thick blanket of jungle treetops. I assumed that it was too dense to land anywhere in the area, but the chopper pilots found a small meadow surrounded by trees and dropped into shoulder-high grass. It was the fastest approach I had been a part of or had witnessed, and I had the feeling that we were crashing, but our pilot set us down smoothly. We quickly jumped out and hustled away from the choppers. After going approximately thirty meters, we fell to the ground and pointed our weapons toward the jungle that surrounded us. Once all the choppers departed, someone gave the order to move out. I sighted Captain Nesbitt, who was looking at his map. He glanced up and pointed toward the direction he wanted us to go. We soon entered a dim jungle, where we quickly picked up a dirt trail. My senses were on overdrive as I noticed the animal sounds first. We had irrefutably disturbed some of the jungle's brightest vocalists. There were loud shrieks, muffled hissings, and one jungle animal that was either growling or loudly snoring. Shrieking bird tweets echoed all around us. I felt like I was part of one of the many *Tarzan* episodes I had faithfully watched on Saturday mornings in my early years. [48] Walking into this dark, noisy, unfamiliar, and enemy-inhabited jungle for the first time was extraordinarily fear provoking, so I walked cautiously with the butt of my M16 at my shoulder in the ready position.

5.2. The Ho Chi Minh Trail

After humping for a couple hours, we took a brief break when Bean, aroused by the possible danger he realized he was in, began complaining about his situation. He started saying that he should not have come and that no one could have forced him. I usually listened to Bean without response, knowing that his tendency was to mouth off when frightened or anxious. Pong pleasantly surprised me when he stood up, looked directly down at the sitting Bean and said, "I don't give a rat's ass whether you wanted to be here or not, but when we hit the shit, you better be shooting back. And if you run, I will shoot you in the back myself."

Pong, a tall, muscular man from Alabama, was approaching the end of his one-year tour in Vietnam and was the most recent member of our squad (he had arrived just prior to me). He claimed to have hit plenty of shit while stationed north of us in the Fifth Marines and was reassigned to the First Marines when the Fifth stood down. A lance corporal, he should have had a higher rank, but rumor was that he had decked a sergeant and lost a stripe. He had earned the name Pong because others said the sergeant had bounced on the ground like a Ping-Pong ball. I was glad to have his experience and appreciated his help in the way he lectured Bean. Up to now, Pong had been fairly quiet, but the gravity of our situation brought out his true colors as a marine who was not afraid of confrontation and leadership. He personified the notorious saying used often by marine drill instructors: "When the shit gets tough, I give the shit."

A loud screeching abruptly startled us. It sounded like an animal in the thick brush only meters away. We assumed it to be a monkey or ape, but Roadie immediately shouted that it was a rock ape. We had all heard of rock apes. They were given their nickname because returning marines claimed that there were jungle apes that threw rocks at them. Some described them as a unique type of Sasquatch. Marines were warned not to defend themselves against these jungle beasts by throwing grenades, because the apes would catch the grenades and toss them back. It was always wise to pick and choose what war stories to believe from returning veterans. This story just made me chuckle. Nevertheless, we had obviously disturbed this jungle habitant, and he or she did not sound happy. Roadie continued with his bullshit. "It sounds like a female in heat and looking for a mate. Let's sacrifice Bean and save us."

That broke the ice, and almost everyone laughed, albeit a nervous type of laughter. Mex added, "It might be a *male* seeking Bean." That one brought even louder laughs.

If I could ever find a good thing to say about Bean, it would be that he could dish out the jokes and take them as well. He laughed at both comments and replied something about keeping his pants on the entire time.

It was time to move on, and I put my canteen back on my belt and gave the order to follow the rest of our platoon. The break and jokes did us good, and we seemed more relaxed, although we were still uncertain about the actual nature of our mission and the trouble that loomed ahead of us.

At some point, I realized that we were traveling north on the Ho Chi Minh Trail, a trail used daily by the NVA to move troops and equipment south and to return their wounded home. It would have been impossible to navigate through the triple-canopy rain forest without a path. This was due to the lower canopy, which was made up of tall, fern-type plants with sharp pointed leaves, nettle plants, poison ivy, and thousands of other types of vegetation presenting many colors from multiple shades of green to bright purple. Vines grew everywhere, branching from the ground and reaching far up tall, mossy trees, where they hung and entwined with the upper canopies. We were aware that poisonous snakes, centipedes, and many other creeping menaces that abundantly prevail in a rain forest awaited anyone that wandered off the path and into their smallholdings.

Without this trail, there could be no sense of direction and no way out. Anyone wandering too far into the jungle would have become lost and disoriented within minutes. We chose to stay on the trail, even when taking necessary breaks. Walking on a footpath was against all teachings in stateside classes and by returning veterans, but we had absolutely no alternative. We continued to hump forward on the path that previous marines had dubbed, “Hell’s Pathway.”

After a half-day of humping, Fox Company made camp in a small clearing among some tall trees. It was an area that had been recently cleared—by the NVA—of underbrush. That evening, our squad was chosen to move farther up the trail to protect the rest of the platoon from a potential (if not probable) nighttime surprise assault. We were to watch for anyone trying to sneak down the trail toward our platoon. In candid terms, we would be the early warning system for the rest of the platoon. This was a normal warfare tactic used by marines, potentially sacrificing a few men to warn and protect the masses. I was to move us about a klick and a half north and establish an ambush site. We were to leave just before dusk in order to have enough light to get to our position and set up. I had orders to engage the enemy without hesitation. Lieutenant Timberlake stressed that we were in a “free-kill zone.” I informed my men to take all the ammo they had with them along with one canteen of water, but to leave their other supplies behind. We left in our normal order—Fig (point man), Wheat (bloop man), me (squad leader), Fitz (radioman), and the rest of our squad—ending with Mex as tail-end Charlie. I naïvely left too late, and it got “jungle dark” shortly thereafter as we apprehensively moved through the dark unfamiliar jungle, following a winding path that was slightly more detectable by its lesser shade of black. I stopped after only a half klick at a bend in the path and arranged us in a tight, straight line in the undergrowth on the right side. This enabled everyone to have a clear shot at anyone or anything coming around the bend and toward us. It was a potential friendly-fire death trap for us in the front positions since it was possible for the marines in the back to fire off target and hit us in the back. To help prevent this possibility, I positioned the men nearly shoulder to shoulder. We had to blindly back off the path and into a habitat that we knew was the home to poisonous reptiles and insects, but it was a lesser danger than lying on the open path. I had earlier warned everyone not to make a peep—which they obeyed—until Bean compromised our position when he frantically screamed, “Help, a creepy just crawled over my legs.”

The anger surged inside me. I had taken enough of Bean’s unprofessionalism and big mouth. He was going to get some or all of us killed. We had put up with Bean’s outbursts in the past, but now we were in a place controlled by our enemy, while sitting on a passageway that they had built. The NVA had to know we were there and moving towards them on the one-and-only navigable path. In hindsight, it would have been wise to leave Bean in the rear, but it was too late. A chain is only as strong as its weakest link, regardless of the number of links. I crawled over to Bean and furiously whispered that he would be returning to our base camp alone if he made one more sound. I was not bluffing, and I am sure he knew it. I backed up the entire squad approximately fifty meters and set up a new ambush site in a similar fashion but in the bushes on the opposite side of the path, where we spent the rest of the night.

The only noises after Bean’s outburst were the normal jungle night sounds and the incessant hissing of bugs. During the daylight hours we had several unseen rock apes that seemed to follow alongside us, howling loudly and making screeching sounds. The rock apes, along with chirping and shrieking birds, quieted down after dark, but I had gotten so used to ignoring them that I barely noticed they were silent. The thick triple canopy of leaves from the trees and vines completely concealed us from the night sky, immersing us in total darkness deep inside this wild jungle. I was lying in a prone position, camouflaged in the thick, tall weeds, waiting for the NVA to move toward us. Although I could not see into the pitch-black wilderness in front of me, I listened for every sound. I was not familiar with the habits of animals and birds in a rain forest, and I regretted not knowing the behaviors of nocturnal animals whose vocal exchanges could warn us of human movement. I remembered reading that blue jays would warn other inhabitants when unwanted strangers entered a forest back home. Now, when one animal stopped vocalizing for a short spell, I wondered if the silence was indicative of approaching NVA forces. The same was true when a new sound permeated the air. I listened for foot movement but realized that the enemy was probably good at moving silently. I remembered being taught by a Vietnam veteran instructor in stateside infantry training that if you couldn't see the enemy, you could smell them. I had found this to be true whenever I was around the local villagers, especially after they ate. Many of the Vietnamese people smelled like nasty, rotten fish, due to their diet of rice, which they "flavored" with two-day-dead—lying in the sun—foul-smelling fish heads. Therefore, I engaged my sense of smell as a means of early detection.

I held a grenade, with the pin partially pulled, in my right hand during the entire night with two or three others lying beside me. I knew that grenades would be our best defense if the NVA approached since their explosions would not give away our specific position, as flashes from our M16s would do if we fired them first. If we did engage the enemy, it would be a very close battle and easily within a grenade's toss.

I tried to concentrate on the path and noises during the night and not allow my mind to wander. Try as I might, I could not help thinking of dying in this far-away forest without ever seeing my loved ones again. I even thought about what type of beast might devour my remains. I was determined to take at least two gooks with me, dying a two-to-one victor. As thoughts jumped through my mind, they gave me a second wind against sleep. The more I thought, the more confident I became that we were not going to die out there. I went into full-combat approach. I remembered something Ski had said in his bullshit session: "You must believe in your fellow marines and maintain your toughness in combat. Think ahead." I became determined to keep us alive, and my thoughts returned to my responsibilities and the accompanying gung-ho courage. It did not matter what awaited us. We would be ready with M16s and grenades as trained. As grunts, our primary purpose in war was to kill the enemy. Come on down your trail, fish breaths!

I stayed awake all night without any further incidents, and the following morning we returned down the trail to get our gear and move back up with the rest of our platoon (there was no time for breakfast). As we returned on the same pathway as the night before, I was dumbfounded to see camouflaged bunkers at every bend. Shockingly, we had naïvely walked past them going up the trail in the dark and later while returning in the early haze of the morning. They were small, deep, one- and two-man foxholes hidden so well from sight that we had to be within a few feet to spot them. Had just one of them been manned by an NVA with an AK-47 rifle (capable of six-hundred rounds per minute),[49] we could have all been mowed down before we could have even determined his location. We now realized that there were going to be enemy bunkers at every turn of the curvy Ho Chi Minh Trail. Even though we knew where to look, we could not discern their locations until we became flush with them or passed them and looked to the side or back behind us.

As we continued, we passed a large mound of medium-sized orange-colored fire ants just off the path. There had to be millions of them, crawling on their mound and the trees and bushes next to it. I stopped to look at one on a limb about eye height. It had huge bug eyes, pincers, and long, hairy legs. For a brief few seconds we stared at each other. I was the one intimidated, and quickly moved on. I thought of how fortunate we were that we did not back into a mound of them the night before when we moved off the path and into our ambush setting—twice.

I had been awake for more than twenty-four hours and wearily trudged along, drenched from the rain forest's humidity, hungry, and weighted down by my gear, including the extra ammo and rations. Fortunately, we had not been chosen to lead the platoon and were humping along in the middle. After we had been traveling north for five hours, we walked into a clearing and were shocked to discover that we were inside an enemy base camp. To our surprise and good fortune, it had been recently abandoned.

The lieutenant instructed me to take my squad and establish security on the ridge side of what now became our encampment. As I approached the ridge, I spotted a mountain stream that, along with large boulders, created a seam through the jungle foliage. It was the most beautiful display of nature I had ever seen, including the view from my trip to the top of the Marble Mountains. Fitz and I dug our foxhole near the only path leading down the ridge and overlooking the picturesque view. My first team dug in to our right and the second and third to our left. I sat down and grabbed some food from my rucksack, took off my boots and socks, and relaxed. A short time later, a marine from one of the other squads approached me. "The lieutenant wants to see you," he said.

"Take your men down that gully and along the river for about two to three miles," Lieutenant Timberlake said as he nodded toward our route. The lieutenant knew not to point because it could be telling an observant enemy where to set up an ambush and await us. "There's a wide opening in the landscape that we can see from here, so go at least that far. Be careful; they could be anywhere out there."

We packed only what we thought we might need, including lots of ammo, and left the rest of our gear behind (a.k.a. "a light load"). Our squad seemed to be the one picked for the most dangerous missions. Mex referred to us as "the expendables," but that would describe most of the soldiers in Vietnam. I realized that two to three miles was a long way from reinforcements. The entire trip was downhill, and I instructed Fig to stop every couple of minutes so we could observe the terrain ahead and around us and look for signs of the enemy. I moved to second in line behind Fig so I could help navigate the route. We were now outside of the rain forest and did not have to follow a path. It was mid-afternoon, affording us plenty of daylight and enabling us to move cautiously, as Fig zigged and zagged around boulders that were two stories high or taller, and surrounded by heavy brush. Approximately halfway to our destination, we spotted a waterfall, plunging over the mountainside and into a small lake below. It was a little off course, but I nodded to Fig to head that way.

As marines who subsisted in the bush, we were accustomed to taking advantage of natural waterways. I divided our squad into two groups, and each group took turn swimming and standing guard for the other. The mountain water rolled over the falls and created a small mist. The squad enjoyed the cool mountain drinking water, a shower, and a bath at the same time. I decided not to partake, being too worried that we would come under fire and I would literally be caught with my pants off, but I took off my shirt and washed up using it as a washcloth.

Once everyone was finished and clothed, I deviated from our mission to travel to the lower opening of the canyon. We had been walking on the side of a mountain and heading downhill and were now approximately five-hundred meters from the canyon stream and triple that distance from the peak. While I was standing watch at the swimming hole, I decided that we would have a greater advantage against the enemy if we moved the patrol uphill. This would enable us to shoot and throw grenades downhill at the NVA if we got into a firefight with them. Changing our direction would throw off any enemy watching and anticipating our route. Lieutenant Timberlake's earlier statement that half of us could be dead by now weighed heavily on my mind as I cautiously contemplated every change in direction. I certainly did not want to lead my squad into trouble, and everywhere was a potential enemy trap. If the NVA outnumbered us so heavily, walking into their ambush would likely be the end of all of us. Going high would also enable us to return to our base camp using a different route than we had used going out. However, if my change in direction led us into an enemy ambush, my logic would not matter because we would no longer matter.

It was safer to travel in the open or river areas than in vegetated areas, where the NVA could appear out of well-concealed spider holes in a coordinated attack. I learned this valuable information from Sergeant Ski when a few of us stayed to bullshit with him after his class lesson in the States. He had told us that his squad was moving up a forested hill when gooks gunned many of them down. The attack came unexpectedly because his fire-support base had just bombed the area with mortar rounds. Unbeknownst to Ski's squad at the time, the enemy had been well protected and concealed underground during the bombings. As Sergeant Ski's squad approached the peak, gooks popped out of spider holes, some only ten meters away from them. The marines had no choice but to rapidly retreat, dragging their wounded with them and leaving their dead behind. Ski said that they had regrouped, medevaced the wounded, and waited for reinforcements, who later took the hill and recovered their dead.

Fig continued to warily lead us upward until we were near the peak. Part of what I learned in Scout Sniper School was to never travel on the peak of a mountain or hill where your silhouettes can easily be spotted from either side. Therefore, I stopped Fig about ten meters short of the top and set up in the shadows and shade of some large boulders. It was an ideal spot that gave us a clear view in most directions. I kept three men awake overlooking key outlets while the rest took turns taking much-needed naps, including me. We had been awake the entire night before when we were camped on the Ho Chi Minh Trail, and we were weary from the lack of sleep and the long journey through the hot and humid rain forest earlier that day. After a couple of hours—with everyone still alive, clean, and rested—we headed toward our base camp.

5.3. Skulls and Bones

While we were patrolling, swimming, and sleeping, Corporal Stevens's squad, along with a corpsman and a Kit Carson scout, were sent on a mission to patrol a path east of us, where they came upon a very odd discovery. Just off their path were two human skulls, human bones, parts of US and foreign ordnances including PRC-25 radio parts, M14 parts, and a Chinese-made gas mask. They also found remnants of a marine or army shirt and M16 shell casings. Some of the bones were partially buried, and there appeared to be some freshly dug graves. The Kit Carson scout told Stevens that a recon team had disappeared in the area in 1968 when their helicopter was shot down. Lieutenant Timberlake instructed Stevens—via the radio—to dig up every possible grave and verify that there were no American bodies entombed there. They were also to attempt to find the rank and possible intelligence information from each body.

Corporal Stevens and his men started digging with their Ka-Bar knives when one of his men, Lance Corporal Rube (not his real name), spotted something in the dirt. He grabbed it with his hand, coming up with a handful of slimy, partially decomposed, and smelly flesh. Rube started cursing as he wiped his hand on anything he could find while the rest of the men laughed. After the jesting died down, the men helped pull the body out of the grave. It was partially bound in an American parachute, and upon unwrapping it, they found a young Asian man dressed in an NVA uniform with no rank or insignias. He had no papers, pictures, or identification and appeared to not have any combat wounds. The corpsman decided that he most likely had suffered a clinical death—possibly malaria and had been dead for two to three weeks. Other sites that appeared to be graves were explored in the same way as the first one, but they were empty. It was strange to us that the North Vietnamese did not send their dead back up the Ho Chi Minh Trail to their loved ones.

Soldiers can develop a twisted sense of humor while serving in a war zone. We could argue that it was part of our mental survival and a way to lessen the impact of the violent and gruesome events that we experienced. Digging up dead gooks would not normally be entertaining, but this happened to be one of those warped-sense-of-humor days, and it was a welcome relief from the fear that had gripped everyone on this mission. One of Stevens's men mounted one of the skulls on a stick, and various soldiers took turns posing with it for a camera that one of his men, who had ignored the forbidden camera ban, brought with him. I always admired Paul Stevens's brash attitude. Per the American Standards of Combat, we were not allowed to film anything dead, including animals. Paul was on his second tour in Vietnam and an excellent leader. He had survived nearly two tours in a war where soldiers sometimes took their own liberties. Paul was always more relaxed and confident than the rest of us and commanded a group of men who followed and respected him implicitly. The men felt that this was weird but harmless humor.

When finished digging, the original body was placed back into its final resting place. Everyone returned to the enemy base camp that we had bizarrely taken over as ours. Some of our fellow marines had discovered caches of rice and corn and were in the process of burning it. There was no reason to leave our enemy raw food, so we cooked it for them.

Fast-forward forty-five years: The "classic" picture of Stevens posing with the skull surfaced on the website of the 2nd Battalion 1st Marines in Vietnam. After seeing the picture of the skull and remembering the strange circumstances surrounding it, I began to question whether it really had been an Asian skull (the corpsman on-site had said it was Asian). Why would the NVA troops leave the skeletal remains of their own men lying out in the open? What if this skull had belonged to an

American soldier on the recon mission in that area that had disappeared three years prior to our mission? Could forensic anthropologists identify a skull's nationality from a picture? If it was an American's skull, could they identify the person from pictures of those who were on the recon chopper? If it was an Asian skull, could it have been one of the South Vietnamese soldiers who had disappeared on the same recon chopper? I felt that this was a matter for the Defense POW/MIA Accounting Agency of the US government in Washington, DC, and sent them notification, with the details, as I knew them. The request quickly gained a life of its own as I received a call from one of their agents, William H. Newell III, requesting more information, particularly the coordinates of the mission and the possible sight. He asked if I was willing to lead an expedition back to the jungle and search for remains.

Thoughts of our missing brothers trigger heartfelt lumps in the throats of veterans. Their remains deserve to be found, and their families should have closure. Of course, I would do anything that may possibly bring about closure to one or more of their families. However, I explained that we had not been at the location documented in military records and the reasons why. There were a few landmarks that might help me to identify the area if we could find them, and I had pictures of a waterfall and some rock formations (Fitz had taken his camera also).

I began contacting some of the guys that that were on the same operation to see if they took any photos, but all of them said they did not and mentioned that we were not supposed to have cameras. Each time I contacted someone it led to more referrals, as everyone wanted to help.

I further contacted the Department of Anthropology at The Ohio State University and after explaining the situation, I asked the following questions:

Can your department study a photo of a skull and determine if it's Asian, Anglo-Saxon, etc.?

There were friendly Vietnamese soldiers in the downed helicopter. Is it possible to identify the skull using photos of the missing soldiers (American or Vietnamese)?

The Department of Anthropology at Ohio State referred me to the POW/MIA office, which I had already contacted, and the American Academy of Forensic Sciences.

In the meantime, my research revealed that a recon team in an H-34 Sikorsky helicopter containing three Army Green Berets and four South Vietnamese troops was shot down on May 20, 1968 near the A Shau Valley, four miles inside Laos near the Ho Chi Minh Trail. As of June 14, 2015, they were still missing.[50]

I sent this information to Mr. Newell, who found some discrepancies between our findings on the trail and the incident in question, including the fact that the soldiers in the H-34 did not have an M14 rifle on board. However, he said that there had been another helicopter crash in which the last-known position was within that general area in Laos. Mr. Newell reported, "The remains and description you provided do tend to match that loss better. I am happy to say that in 2003 a recovery team recovered enough remains to account for all of the missing from that incident. In the end, however, even if you could lead a team back to the general location your patrol observed the skull; it is unlikely we could ever get you to that general area without a more accurate description in broader terms of where you were. If you do find additional information that could get us to that point, please let me know."

That is where the search ended, but only temporarily. As Mr. Newell suggested, I am still searching for additional information, including seeking a forensic anthropologist that can determine a skull's genetics from a photograph. According to the Joint Task Force-Full Accounting in Hawaii of the helicopter crash mentioned by Mr. Newell, human skulls were not part of the remains discovered in 2003.[51]

Note: As of February 2018, there were still 1,602 Americans missing from the Vietnam War.[52]

5.4. Still Alive

By now it had been two days since we dropped into enemy territory, and we felt relatively safe in our secure site. It was obvious why the NVA had picked this spot as a camp. Approximately a third of the encampment rested on a cliff. Thick jungle protected the rest of the area. There were only two paths leading into the compound that we had to watch particularly well. Toward evening, an NVA soldier was shot in the head and killed when he was spotted walking down one of the paths toward our base camp. It was somewhat alarming that he had been able to get as close as he had, with full gear and an AK-47 rifle, before someone recognized him as an NVA soldier. Since he was alone, it appeared that he had been on watch duty or was a solitary scout and was returning, unaware that we had taken over his home base.

On our second night of the mission, termed Scott Orchard, we were able to share guard duty and catch up on much-needed sleep. For the rest of the mission, we continued to go on patrols starting on the same path and then branching off into other areas. We did not engage in any more night patrols. One of my squad's daytime missions took us near the highest mountaintop, enabling a bird's-eye view of the area, but not any sightings of our well-hidden enemy. For the entire operation, we knew that the enemy was close by and watching us. Helicopters are noisy and not capable of sneaking troops behind enemy lines without alerting the enemy. They had left items behind—including food and even some small-arms ammunition—in their hasty retreats. After two more days of patrols, our company moved to a high-grass clearing, where helicopters extracted us. Some units reported small arms fire as they lifted off, but all the choppers made it out safely.

Notes: It is still unknown why the enemy did not engage us when we entered their region. They had to know we were there and that we were moving toward them in on their own heavily bunkered trail. It should have been an NVA general's dream. One theory is that their troops had moved out on a mission of their own, and that there were mostly noncombatants that stayed behind. Another one was that they had orders to stand down since we were in the midst of peace talks and the people of North Vietnam, like those of the United States, were weary of war and the deaths of their sons. I also heard that we actually had surprised and intimidated them with all our helicopters coming in at once, causing them to quickly evacuate their bases and take their POWs with them (we did not find any proof that there had been POWs there at that time). For whatever reason, the enemy—with their tails between their legs—hurried away and hid in the bushes.

The American generals wanted confrontations with the enemy prior to reaching a peace agreement. They were running out of time and craved one last battle before we stood down—the kind that results in lots of blood on both sides and additional stars on their lapels. It would not have mattered how many of us got slaughtered in a faraway jungle bloodbath, because they would have simply doubled or tripled our number killed and reported it as the number of enemies killed. Another victory for our side! They rationalized this mission by saying that we were dropping in on the enemy's base camp to rescue our POWs, a politically-correct act of heroism. I have reasoned that the originators of this mission were disappointed that the enemy did not engage us and that there were not lots of casualties. The fact that we all returned alive from such a sizeable and dangerous undertaking was somewhat of a miracle. Sometimes, it's better to be lucky than good.

One more comment on this mission: it was top secret. I am not sure if the enemy found out about the mission on their own (they usually did via the "friendly" local forces), but that does not seem likely or they would have had time to evacuate and take all of their equipment and supplies with them. It was probably a top-secret mission orchestrated by the military but withheld from American politicians who presumed the military brass was obeying their requirements and staying out of the border states of Laos and Cambodia. It also demonstrated indifference by our top military leaders to the public's outcry to stop needless American deaths.

There have been theories that by 1971, the North Vietnamese people, having lost more than one million soldiers,[53] *were pressuring their leaders for peace. Nearly every battle with US forces resulted in their defeat. They had no credible defense against our superior warriors, weapons, and fire support. The facts that our intelligence reported that the NVA were encamped in large numbers and that our evidence showed they had left their base quickly indicates that they had indeed been there. It also suggests that their military leaders were under orders to avoid further casualties, especially since they knew that we were not going to stay in Vietnam and finish the fight. That being said, it is ironic that our military leaders were willing to frivolously sacrifice our lives. President Nixon's administration was in the process of deescalating our troop strength in Vietnam. The military's attempt to engage in one last big battle implies that we had our own warlords who were going to do things their way. We entered the area under the pretense that we were trying to rescue our prisoners of war. Had POWs been there, sending that many soldiers into a jungle (by helicopter) to rescue them would have likely resulted in them being killed. Generals cannot be timid, but recklessness with their troops is shameful.*

Historical records indicate there was no solid basis for the belief that there were American prisoners of war at the base camps the marines invaded in Operation Scott Orchard.[54] The enemy's jungle base camps did retain prisoners at times during the war, and many of these camps had temporary prison cells (bamboo cages) for our POWs prior to moving them north into established camps like the infamous "Hanoi Hilton."

5.5 Hill 785

After returning from Operation Scott Orchard, our platoon boarded early-morning choppers for a flight into another forested area northwest of Da Nang, near an infiltration route that sprouted off the Ho Chi Minh Trail. We were near the neighboring country of Laos, but this time on the Vietnam side and well-fortified on Hill 785, one of the area's higher mountain peaks (the mountainous peaks were given hill designations related to their height). Shortly after landing and spreading out into our positions, we witnessed an amazing spectacle. A Phantom fighter jet began dropping explosives on a small section of the trail.[55] The Phantom came in above us and straight at its target, releasing napalm missiles that exploded upon impact with the ground. The pilot circled around us and bombed the target again. The loud explosions and the huge white clouds of napalm, followed by red balls of fire, rapidly rolled throughout the target area. As quickly as it had appeared, the Phantom safely departed. The smoke continued to rise above the trees, becoming puffy and black until it was eventually blown away by wind.

It is difficult to hit a specific target in a jungle. The entire theater was massive, consisting of hundreds of square miles of mountains and heavy vegetation. A forward observer with high-powered binoculars (who had joined our platoon), guided the pilot to a relatively small area, where the Phantom had an estimated two direct hits, or near hits, on a section of the Ho Chi Minh Trail's infiltration route where he had spotted enemy movement. The impact areas were one-hundred square meters each, or two side-by-side football fields. Anyone within that area would have been incinerated. The enemy soldiers who were near the area probably suffered burn over much of their bodies and died unimaginable deaths. I can only conceive how horrifying it was for the survivors who were fortunate enough to be out of range of these hell bombs to witness the destruction and mutilation.

Napalm (radio call name "barbecue") is a mixture of acids and gasoline that causes horrifying burns to human flesh. The oxygen in the air accelerates the burning.[56] Marines were cautioned that if our bodies got exposed to napalm, we should smother those areas of the skin with mud (to block out oxygen) and await medical evacuation. We had been told that the only treatment for parts of our bodies burned by napalm was to surgically remove all sections of affected flesh.

Note: The horrors of napalm and its collateral damages were highlighted in a 1972 photograph "The Napalm Girl," taken by Nick Ut of the Associated Press. Ut photographed Kim Phuc, a nine-year-old girl, screaming in pain as she went running naked from her village—along with other crying children. Her village had been mistakenly bombed with napalm by South Vietnamese forces, and the little girl suffered burns over one-third of her body. Ut reported that the girl was screaming, "Too hot! Too hot!"[57]

Throughout our first day and night, our forward observer called for mortar rounds from a nearby fire-support base whenever he spotted movement. His targets were always in the same general area where the Phantom jet had dropped the napalm. At night, we spotted dim light, signifying non-stop movement of enemy troops and equipment. In the vast darkness, a small light could be seen for miles. Every time we saw it, our observer determined the coordinates of the light and called for mortar bombardment of the area.

Surrounding us was a vast mountainous wilderness of green foliage, stretching out as far as the naked eye could see. Conspicuous were the barren splotches where American aircraft had earlier destroyed the greenery by dropping the dioxin Agent Orange. These areas were growing back, but were recognizable by smaller growth underneath, accentuated by dead and leafless trees extending high above the grass, similar to the way a year-old forest fire area would appear in forested areas of the United States.

On our second night on Hill 785, the NVA must have had enough of our bombings. They had to know that we were initiating the attacks. It was unknown how many casualties the NVA soldiers suffered, but the Phantom's napalm missiles and ground-to-ground mortar rounds from our fire base were accurate enough to have caused human casualties, destroyed enemy weapons and supplies, and impeded their movements. Two hours after dark, one of our trip flares activated down the hill in front of me, lighting that area and alerting us to a possible sapper.

Note: Sappers were operatives trained by the NVA and Vietcong to infiltrate any position, regardless of how fortified it may be. They were well-trained in camouflage methods, patience, crawling under or removing wire, and the weaknesses of American soldiers while on watch. Although sappers were disadvantaged in numbers, firepower, and technology, they damaged hundreds of military bases, killing and wounding many soldiers in the process.[58]

When we first landed on Hill 785, I was surprised by how protected it was from enemy invasion or incoming mortar rounds. We were told that our engineer battalion had professionally prepared it. The entire perimeter was fortified with sandbag bunkers that were built like underground homes. Double and triple rows of sandbags protected all four sides and their roofs. Small window openings on the slope side of the hill were just large enough for us to rest an M16 on sandbag sills, enabling us to fire from inside the roofed bunkers. In addition, a small doorway led to fortified topless bunkers, where we stood watch. The basic premise was that we could go inside the bunker if we were taking incoming rockets and fight from the roofless bunkers in case of an enemy ground attack. A triple row of razor wire encircled the camp, starting twenty meters down the hill from our bunkers with the last row ending approximately forty meters away. Flares attached to trip wires were concealed throughout the wiring apparatus to guard against sappers.

Only seconds after the first flare was tripped, a second one activated just around the hill from us. I was awake and on watch during this time and did not know how to react. I was not even sure that anyone was trying to infiltrate us. We were used to needing permission to fire, and we were not instructed any differently on this hill. I followed protocol, knowing that we were camped with our company and platoon commanders.

I had not seriously embraced the idea that enemy-trained sappers could crawl under and through our razor wire to penetrate our perimeter at night, because I thought it was inconceivable. To me, it was just another concocted story that had been inflated over time. When I was a boot, it seemed as if I was frequently playing a game of "truth or bullshit" in regard to the war accounts from returning vets and instructors. I never believed in sappers and here I was standing guard at night on Hill 785 in Vietnam being proven wrong—by sappers. I could have been compared to a WWII seaman who did not believe there were kamikaze planes until one crashed into his ship.

In a likely ground assault, and despite the razor wire, trip flares, open Agent-Orange areas, and a steep nighttime climb to our fortified positions, sappers were attempting to infiltrate our perimeter on Hill 785. At least two of them were within twenty to forty meters of us when they tripped the flares. This was not close enough to hit us with a tossed grenade (thrown uphill), which was why the flares were placed in those areas. The next morning, a marine on the side where the second flare had activated said he saw the shadow of an NVA scurrying down the hill. He did not know how to react either. When I asked the lieutenant the following morning, he said we were in a free-fire zone and to shoot at anything that moved down the slope of the hill, and "if any more flares are tripped, unload on the general area with everything you got." I should have already figured this out on my own. There were no villages or inhabitants within miles.

Notes: While I was serving as awards writer, my first sergeant (Top) said there were no longer free-fire zones. He was upset about it because he thought that having to get permission to fire would get marines killed. He was correct; there were no longer free-fire zones. General

Creighton Abrams, who in June 1968 replaced General William Westmoreland as the American commander in Vietnam, did away with them to protect the civilian population. However, soldiers tried to use practical sense to know when to fire first without permission. During my entire time in Vietnam, the question of when to fire was unclear and I always reacted passively when spotting real or perceived enemy movement.

I was anxious to spend more nights in our bunkers, now that I was aware of the situation and ready for any attempt by sappers to infiltrate our fortified perimeter. I was actually looking forward to it. However, after only two days and two nights on Hill 785, we were given orders to evacuate and destroy all the ammunition we could not take with us. There was a fortified ammo dump near the center of our perimeter that sheltered enough explosives to fill a small armory. We could have been under attack for a week and not run out of M16 rounds, machine gun rounds, grenades, LAWs (light antitank weapons), and M79 (blooper) rounds. The sheer amount of these supplies warned of the potential enemy danger on Hill 785. Our job was to dispose of everything except the M16 rounds, which we took with us. We grabbed boxes of grenades and began to toss them, one at a time, down the hill. Others began shooting LAWs and blooper rounds. As I stood back and observed (after throwing a few grenades), I could not believe the danger this posed—with marines standing (instead of kneeling) and tossing hand grenades while their buddies on both sides of them did the same. Many of the marines were throwing grenades like baseballs instead of the standard grenade toss, as we had been taught. In addition, there were some very weak arms, resulting in the explosions being dangerously close. Suddenly, Fig fell back holding his neck. I yelled out for everyone to hold his fire as I ran to the kneeling Fig. He had a piece of corrugated shrapnel the size of a quarter lodged in his neck under his chin. I managed to pull it out, but it was still hot enough to slightly burn my fingers. I yelled for everyone to slow down and throw the grenades farther away from their positions. To my surprise, Fig (with a smirk on his face), ignoring the wound in his neck, went back to his position and began to chuck more grenades. Later, Corporal Stevens got hit with shrapnel from a grenade that he had thrown, which hit a tree branch and exploded just twenty meters from him. Our corpsmen removed it from his neck and, despite the trickles of blood running out of his ear, he also went back to the fun. After destroying thousands of dollars of military ammo, we gathered the rest of our supplies and awaited our choppers.

I was surprised that we vacated Hill 785 with no replacements, because it was a large fortified vantage point for US troops against the NVA. From this position, we could hinder movement of enemy troops and supplies as they flowed down the infiltration route from the Ho Chi Minh Trail. They were on their way to battle US, South Vietnamese, and Korean troops, as well as other enemy combatants. Our napalm bombs and mortar rounds established our superiority and had to have had an intimidating effect, keeping the enemy on the defensive. This small, two-day mission was perhaps the most important of all of the operations I witnessed during my tour of duty in Vietnam. It genuinely had a productive purpose—until we abandoned this strategic hill.

Notes: Approximately eighteen-million gallons of the herbicide Agent Orange were sprayed over mostly forested areas of South Vietnam from 1962 through 1971. As many as four-hundred thousand South Vietnamese people were killed or maimed from the aftereffects, and five-hundred thousand children suffered birth defects (as later estimated by the Vietnamese government).[59]

The US Department of Veterans Affairs recognizes at least fifty illnesses/diseases connected to Agent Orange that affected Vietnam veterans and their children, resulting in serious health concerns and death. A partial list includes: type II diabetes; Hodgkin's disease; heart disease; Parkinson's disease; thirty-eight types of cancer, including malignant throat and trachea cancers, breast and skin cancers, brain cancer, several types of leukemia, malignant bone and muscle cancers; and birth defects including spina bifida (spinal cord), congenital heart disease, cleft palate, webbed fingers, a type of dwarfism, thyroid defects, and so on.[60]

Cpl. Stevens near Ho Chi Minh Trail in Laos
Photo: Paul Stevens

Operation Scott Orchard; Cpl. Gerhardt patrolling 2nd (no helmet) **Photo: Les Fitzgerald**

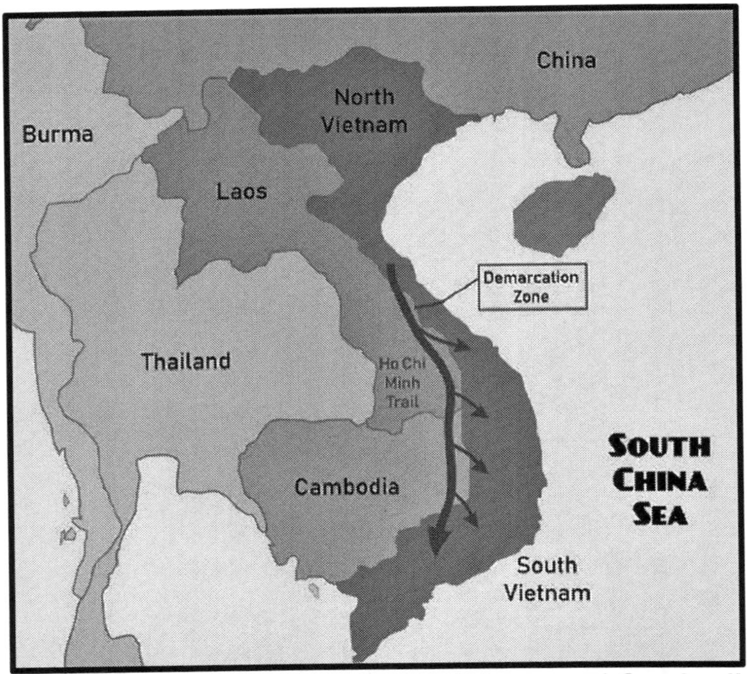

The Ho Chi Minh Trail ran through Laos and Cambodia and was used daily by the North to stage and move troops and equipment south **Drawing: Lee Van Mora**

Vietcong tunnel system with entry points from hamlet and river **Drawing: Lee Van Mora**

Renowned picture by Nick Ut entitled "Napalm Girl" (Associated Press June 8, 1972) that captured the pain and terror of Phan Thi Kim Phuc escaping her village after an accidental aerial napalm attack by friendly South Vietnamese forces (shown in background). Ut said the 9-year-old child was screaming, "too hot, too hot."

AP Photo/Nick Ut

Part VI

★★★

6.1 Short

The Marine Corps announced the date that we would be pulling out of Vietnam, and instantly we were all "short." Since my first month in Vietnam, I had been looking forward to the day I would leave. The urge to go home grew as time passed and as I experienced the inhumane parts of war, in addition to the daily incidental battles with mosquitoes, heat, humidity, and leadership challenges. In spite of daily personal-hygiene habits, there were times when everything was filthy, including us. The water, especially in some rice paddies, was contaminated with human and water buffalo feces. Between the muck and grime of the foxholes, the high humidity, the scarcity of clean water to bathe, and our filthy clothing, we reeked of odor similar to a jungle monkey. When we ran out of supplied water, we filled our canteens with the clearest water we could find, added a couple of purification tablets, shook it, and waited a half hour before drinking it or washing our face with it. Dysentery was common and something we all tolerated at times. Sometimes, the best part of our week was being close enough to a river during the daytime so that we could swim and bathe.

Prior to joining the Marine Corps, I was a young man pretending to know more about life than I did, and I believed my future was in my hands. Shortly thereafter, I was in Vietnam and the only sure thing in my hands was an M16 rifle. My future depended on luck, some skill, and the willingness to kill other young people before they killed me. A young person generally takes living for granted, until one day when his or her country goes to war. Goals, dreams, relationships, and other ambitions are no longer taken for granted as he or she realizes that life could be snatched away at any moment. Surroundings, ways of thinking, values, and outlook rapidly change, adding a new dimension to his or her development. The size of his or her world expands from a neighborhood to a planet. Interests go from self-absorbed comfort zones to political actions that now disturb an awakening of the soul, intensifying the natural confusion of early adulthood. I was experiencing such an evolution. A period of time defined by war, assassinations of public figures, riots and unrest are later recognized as historical times. The years 1964 through 1972 were the epic years of the Vietnam/baby boomer generation.

My future would soon be back under my control. Now that I was short, I worried more than ever about my responsibility to bring everyone home safely. No one wanted to die, but it was particularly sad when a comrade was killed in his last few weeks of duty. US ground operations were causing a lot of American casualties. Was this the right strategy? Similar to the way wars were fought as far back as biblical times, we were to find and engage. However, the early historic battles were quite different from ours. One primary difference was our weapons, replacing swords and shields with our automatic rifles and bombs. Another difference was the size of the battles. Ours in Vietnam were mere skirmishes compared to many of the huge ancient battles, where the victor claimed property and long-term standing. In Vietnam, winning a skirmish meant very little and did not affect the enemy's resolve. If we took casualties, our small victory could have negative reactions at home. Similar to a football team that repeatedly runs off right tackle with cheerless results, ground operations continued throughout the war with little or no change. Although we were all short, our nightly patrols and ambushes continued as in the past, and I sandbagged all of them, with one exception—a last mission to the Han.

We were familiar with this exercise—set a night ambush on the river. We never sandbagged river ambushes—probably because it would be difficult to explain that you thought you were on a riverbank if caught in the middle of a rice paddy. I positioned the squad in a straight line on a high bank overlooking a bend in the river. We had become proficient at taking turns on watch with only two of us awake while everyone else slept. Near the end of my watch, around 2300, I spotted movement on the river close to our bank. It appeared to be a small rowboat or raft. I tapped the guys around me as I called it in. To my surprise, I got immediate permission to fire, and we lit it up, firing into the river with our M16s and tossing hand grenades over the bank (the sighting was too close for the grenade launcher). The bank was approximately twenty feet high, and the movement disappeared into the brush between the water and us. We stopped firing after a couple of minutes (I fired only two magazines of twenty rounds each) and Wheat shot sunshine from his M79 over the river. Shortly after the firing stopped, the lieutenant called me wanting a casualty report. I replied that we were all OK and no enemy bodies had been spotted, but there might be some. He advised that we were to move downstream closer to the water to watch for floating bodies or wounded VC trying to escape. I moved us about fifty meters into a location where we could see down the bank, where the water met land without being blocked by brush, but not any closer to the river. I was not about to lose anyone looking for dead or wounded VC as memories crowded my mind of the two marines who had drowned in the river doing just that. After approximately an hour of no additional sightings, we were given orders to return to our platoon.

Note: It never made a lot of sense to me that our river sightings and ambushes rarely resulted in finding enemy bodies. I later discovered that the VC's tunnel system stretched to areas of the rivers where they were able to find a safe haven and doctor the wounded.

On one of our final nights in the bush, our platoon was camped near the banks of the river. Our squad was to protect the perimeter of our compound while Stevens and Cracker's squads went on ambush patrols. This was always a welcome duty since we were able to grab more sleep before it got dark. However, just after dusk, Lieutenant Timberlake sent Fitz and me on a two-man killer team overlooking an inlet off the Han River. It was the first time I had heard of a two-man killer team, other than in reference to a two-man sniper team that consisted of the sniper and his spotter. The lieutenant wanted a small team to move into a particular ambush site with a lower risk of being detected. He told us to find a cove that he showed me on his map. Intel reported the existence of rowboats at the site that they suspected were being used by the Vietcong to move supplies down river. Lieutenant Timberlake told us to kill as many VC as possible and then "get the hell out of there and back here."

Fitz and I moved slowly through the thick brush that ran laterally along the river, cautiously staying off the trail that would have made our travel easier but was booby-trap risky. The inlet was five klicks away from our platoon's perimeter and easy to find because it cut off our travel along the river. We cautiously slipped inland and set up on a ledge overlooking a cove with shallow water. There were two small canoe-style boats lying upside down on the bank. We were both tired from being on patrol the night before and humping most the day to our platoon's current compound. In addition, Staff Sergeant Beck had called a squad-leader meeting that interrupted a short nap I had attempted in the early evening.

Fitz and I decided to split watch. He took first watch, and I immediately fell into a deep sleep, not caring about where I was or the potential danger. For grunts in

Vietnam, sleep sometimes overrode the worry of getting killed. During these times, we often snoozed through what had become customary nighttime war sounds, such as another squad's firefight, mortar rounds launching and exploding in the distance, or choppers flying medevac missions. Sounds traveled longer distances at night, but if these sounds woke us and there was no immediate threat or a need for our support, most of the time we went back to sleep. Fitz woke me when it was my turn to keep watch, and he fell asleep. At some point during my watch, I fell back asleep! This was an unforgivable offense in the marines, whether in a war zone or stateside. It was not unusual to fall asleep on watch due to the common sleep deprivation brought on by wakeful days and nights, but it was easy to get caught. When on ambush watch, the platoon radioman checked with all deployed squads every ten to fifteen minutes. Our platoon radioman, Corporal Horn (Horny), was vainly trying to call me. He could have (and should have) awakened our lieutenant, who would have likely sent a squad to check on us. I would have possibly lost one of my hard-earned stripes. Horny was a friend I had met in Okinawa during our staging time there. During the day, I had made the comment to him that I wished that I could just get a half hour of sleep. Staff Sergeant Beck had continually interrupted the squad leaders for his usual trivial meetings that always accentuated his stupidity. He did not have to stay up on watch at night and was always awake during the day. Due to his incompetence, he could not recognize the importance of a few hours' sleep, the lack of which could lead to poor decisions and accidents. His "briefings" included handing out boxes of C rats to each squad (which only squad leaders could accept) and repeating whatever he had told us in the days and weeks prior. Sometimes in his "meeting," Stevens and I would exchange glances of perplexity that this idiot could actually be second in command (to Lieutenant Timberlake) of our platoon in an actual war theater. It would have been necessary to double his IQ to equal any one of the other marines in our entire platoon.

The most incompetent and embarrassing display of Staff Sergeant Beck's contrived authority were the times he attempted to communicate on the field radio, always misidentifying himself as "Fox Six." This was the company commander's handle, but he thought it was his. He would start out, "Da, Fox Six here," and then continue with something really stupid like "I, I, uh, want squad leads to call radio if you see Charlie."

What did he think we would do? Keep it a secret? He had been in the marines for sixteen years and had only climbed to the rank of staff sergeant (E-6). After the war, the marines removed (forced out) these "lifer" staff sergeants who were not capable of ever ascending to the rank of E-7 or above. There were quite a few of them.

Horny was well aware of Staff Sergeant Beck's shortcomings and their effects on the squad leaders. He realized that I had fallen asleep and did not overreact. After about a half hour, I awoke and quickly called in my ten-minute "all clear." We both kept it quiet and did not tell anyone—not even Fitz, who snoozed through the entire ordeal. Thank you, Horny!

Fast-forward forty-four years to when I visited Fitz and his wife, Mary, for the first time at their warm homestead in Washington State:

"By the way, Fitz, remember that two-man killer team we were on toward the end of our tour?"

"Yeah. We were really hung out there, just the two of us."

"Well, old buddy, there's something I've been meaning to tell you. You see, I fell asleep on my watch that night, leaving both of us snoozing."

"Huh? Now I find out about this shit."

We both have laughed about it ever since, and I sarcastically remind him, "Fitz, sometimes it's better to be lucky than good." I had better not print his reply.

Note: Fitz faced plenty of danger during his time as the radioman. In addition to being the tallest man in our squad, he humped a radio with an antenna projecting five to six feet above his head. The antenna was easy to spot, making him a likely target for an enemy sniper. It was wise on my part to wait forty-four years to tell the big guy about the additional danger that I had put him in when I dozed off on our two-man killer team.

The following evening, Lieutenant Timberlake gave me an order to hump to an army outpost approximately two miles away and give their commander a verbal message. He assigned a marine from one of the other squads to go with me, but we did not take a radio. I was to tell their lieutenant that we were going to patrol in their tactical area of responsibility that night but would stay at least one klick away from their post. Lieutenant Timberlake did not want to offer that information over the radio.

We left immediately in order to return before dark. As we neared the post, two army soldiers recognized us as marines and came out to greet us. Marines were easily identified by the camouflaged khakis we wore as compared to the olive-green ones worn by the army soldiers. "We heard that the marines had already left Vietnam," one of them said. "Do you guys really camp outside all the time?"

The Army was taking over our tactical area of operation and doing it their way—by constructing fortified outposts with sandbag bunkers, encircled with razor wire.

They would run their patrols from there. This contrasted greatly with the Marines. We were basically nomads living in the bush, moving our perimeter most nights and digging our own foxholes with no sandbags. We had a saying, “Home is where we dig it.”

As I entered their compound, we were joined by about two-dozen soldiers, who began asking questions. They wanted to know about their new area of responsibility and the hot spots. Once I began, I found that I had a lot to say. I warned of the obvious dangers of booby traps, night ambushes, and snipers. I also warned them to be vigilant and never assume that the enemy was not out there or not watching them. “Even though you may never see him, Charlie’s out there, and don’t ever let your guard down.” I used the examples of the marine who got shot for lighting a cigarette when he thought it was safe, and the night that I stood up while on watch and was sniped at. After a while, I realized it was getting dark and quickly found the lieutenant and delivered our message. The army lieutenant was also curious about his new territory and asked a lot of similar questions; wanting to know the danger areas and ways we had taken casualties. Unfortunately, I had not brought my map, which I had marked with our previous patrols, but I answered his inquiries as well as I could. The two of us left just after dark and returned to our position without incident. I remembered those first weeks as a squad leader and how green I had been, but I was proud that I was now combat-tested and eager to share my knowledge and wisdom with our replacements, as Sergeant Ski had done when I was a boot. I said a prayer that my new army friends would get home safely.

Later that night, we left on our last, and unusually late (0200), ambush patrol. Some of the guys wanted to fake a firefight to make the last patrol our “Grand finale.” It would have been nice to put an exclamation point on surviving our time in Vietnam, but I had learned that anytime someone discharged his weapon, other marines or civilians could get hurt. All I had to say was no. We had developed into a cohesive unit that no longer squabbled for the mere sake of it. The turning points for members of our squad was the firefight in the Arizonas, where we had all fought as a unit; and our harrowing experiences in Laos, where the squad had trusted my decisions. Bullets whizzing close by them in the Arizonas and the overwhelming fear of death, particularly when the thirteen of us guarded a section of the Ho Chi Minh trail at night, made them take the war and their survival seriously.

The following evening, we moved our location for our final two nights in the bush. We camped next to the Han River, where we dug foxholes in a tight perimeter. It was our turn to stay in while Corporal Stevens and Sergeant Cracker's squads went separate ways. It began to rain and then to storm. The moonlight could not get through the thick clouds. Our foxhole faced west, and the rain came at us horizontally. It was my most vigilant night in Southeast Asia, with the exception of our mission in Laos. All I could think of was that I had fewer than forty-eight hours to go, and I could not allow sappers to follow the rain into our perimeter. With my bush hat pulled down to just above my eyes, I stayed awake the entire night—forgoing my time to sleep and waiting one last time for a visit from Charlie. Luckily for him, he disappointed me. I realized that I was no longer gung-ho but instead felt a genuine hatred for our enemy, and I wanted some more payback before my departure.

The following day, we had an unexpected visitor: General Davis, the assistant commandant of the Marine Corps and a four-star general. He had flown into the country and taken a chopper to share a last meal in the bush with the last combat marines. I was surprised to see that he did not bring additional protection with him, until I realized *we* were his security. He packed the typical officer's .45-caliber revolver on his belt. I was assigned to sniper-watch while he was there. The only potential threat was a small forest approximately a half klick to the west. I stood outside the perimeter by the foxhole that was nearest the forest with my M16 on my shoulder in a ready position. That small assignment was my last combat exercise.

After General Davis left, Lieutenant Timberlake called my name. The platoon commander generally occupied space in the center of the encampment. This served as the field headquarters and was also the place where the platoon sergeant and radioman camped. All other marines were on the outside perimeter, creating a circle similar to how a wagon train circled its wagons to fight off an attack by "Indians" in western movies. Lieutenant Timberlake was standing as I approached. "Gerhardt, you are receiving a combat promotion to sergeant and will take over as the Fox Company office manager when we leave for the rear tomorrow. It will be your responsibility to see that all our personnel, their records, and anything else that belongs to our company gets packed and shipped back to the world."

"Yes, sir; thank you, sir." I was at a loss for words.

"You deserve it, marine. Good luck." The lieutenant gave me a rare smile and moved on to other business.

I knew that Lieutenant Timberlake had a lot to do with my promotion. I had a rocky start as a squad leader but felt that I had eventually earned his respect and become someone he could count on. I also knew that we were lucky to have had a platoon commander with such considerable experience and leadership. I went back to my position with a rare feeling of achievement.

On our last night, all squads stayed in as we took our normal turns on perimeter watch, but I, ironically, did not feel sleepy—even when not on my watch. My wandering thoughts kept me awake. It was time to end this chapter of my life, but I did not want to turn the page yet—at least not until I prepared myself for it. I thought about seeing my family, my buddies, maybe my old girlfriend who had stopped writing months ago, and watching the Buckeyes play football again. I wondered if my pre-Vietnam personality and sense of humor would return. The sky and its shimmering stars were beautiful that final night, and at some point, I fell asleep.

Note: I believe my personality and sense of humor returned to me, which among other things, enabled me to forget what's-her-face.

Early mornings were my favorite times, and my last one was no different. The distant mountains gradually appeared through the light-blue haziness of morning dew, like a slow-developing photo in a darkroom. I had a cool and damp feeling that reminded me of awakening outdoors at my summer campsite in the woods behind our house. There was plenty of time to open a C-rat can for breakfast, using the P-38 can opener (referred to as a "John Wayne") that I always carried around my neck on an extra dog tag chain. In my canteen cup, I mixed a packet of hot cocoa with water from my canteen, warming it with a chunk of C-4 (plastic explosive) that I lit with my Zippo lighter. I had breakfast and then smoked a couple Marlboro cigarettes left from one of my C-ration packs and relaxed—the stress of being a combat squad leader was all but over.

6.2. Goodbye, Vietnam

I awaited my last chopper ride in Vietnam. It was a typical hot mid-afternoon day. As always, the humidity was high but hardly noticeable now that I was accustomed to it. In the distant blue sky, I saw them. The blessed choppers were coming to take us away for our long-anticipated journey home. We were leaving the bush for the rear and would soon be back in the world. I heard the accustomed *whop*, *whop*, *whop* of their blades as they approached from the open rice paddy to our north. Corporal Stalzer, our company radioman, popped multiple smoke grenades—one of every color—to guide them to the landing zone and to celebrate our last chopper extraction.

As I waited for my squad to load, I looked around a last time. We were camped next to the Han River, just upstream from where two comrades had drowned in its robust current, where I had "blooped" the opposite bank, and near where we had taken part in night patrols, firefights, and ambush settings, including a two-man killer team. I glanced at our abandoned perimeter, surrounded by the barren dirt of foxholes we had dug two evenings prior and restored that morning. The booby traps, firefights, snipers, rocket attacks, gooks, snakes, and even my mosquito blood sisters would soon be memories. We proudly boarded our chopper as the last fighting marines in Vietnam. I observed the courageous crew. They were probably nearing their time to stand down also. The gunners, one on each side, were manning .60-caliber machine guns as they intensely watched the landscape in full-ready mode. We sat in our accustomed way on each side of the chopper with M16s between our legs and facing up. The pilot lifted off and quickly gained altitude. The machine gunners relaxed, and I stood up to look out the gunner's opening on the port side. I could see the locals with umbrella straw hats working their rice paddies, a few water buffaloes, and the Marble Mountains. I turned and exchanged glances with a few members of my squad. There were some half smiles on their combat-toughened faces. I glanced at Fitz, but he just stared ahead, seemingly lost in thought with a faraway look on his face. He later told me that he was in a state of disbelief that this was really happening. It was too noisy to talk in a chopper, but some of us exchanged nods that conveyed our thoughts better than spoken words ever could have. We were the fortunate ones, about to go home safely. As we methodically disembarked, there was no cheering or high fives. We were too professional—too seasoned for the juvenile behaviors we would have engaged in just one year prior. We were leaving the blood of some of our brothers behind. We instinctively understood that we would never be capable of celebrating our time in the Republic of South Vietnam, even though we would perpetually reminisce about each day we were there. We were everlastingly and coherently bonded as brothers of war.

Epilogue

6.3 Coming Home to Groveport, Ohio

I was classified by my unit as "key personnel" and not allowed to take immediate leave once back in the world. Now a sergeant and our platoon's office manager, I was directed to stay until everyone and everything was "in order." This lasted about sixty days, and then, in my gleaming, spit-shined boots, I took ten days' leave. I had called my parents earlier in the week and told them that I was coming home but did not know the flight times yet. However, I communicated the wrong day and arrived a day later than what I had indicated. My parents, who both worked outside the home, took that entire day off work (the day before my arrival) and waited for me at the Port Columbus International Airport. That was a time when I had no telephone contact. I still feel saddened about misleading my beloved parents. I picture them waiting for me, sighting other soldiers about my height and build, and thinking on each occasion that it was I—only to be disappointed time and time again. They finally went home once the last flight emptied for the night. The following day, I called them from the airport, and they hurried there to greet me. My journey was over; it felt great to be home. I was as I had left—a proud American.

Afterword

6.4 Vietnam the Countryside

War is hell, but this small fragment of God's green earth was only occupied short term by the war devil. Located on the South China Sea, with China Beach, mountains, a green oasis of jungles, winding rivers, and rice paddies, Vietnam soon recouped its natural beauty. A soldier cannot grasp the splendor of a land when at war upon it.

6.5 Lost Brothers

There is a common wartime belief that a soldier should not get too close to other soldiers for fear that they might die, and thus emotionally affect him or her too much. I disagree with this type of thought. The real bond between comrades is what makes a combat squad a safer unit. Once you are in a combat zone, your thoughts shift from fighting for country, or whatever else your reason for being there might be, to fighting to protect one another. This is what builds a cohesive team. Your brothers are there to protect your life, and you theirs. As you share your life, family, pets, or girlfriend (share as in your fondness for her—ha ha), this security bond becomes stronger.

Mourning our lost comrades is the worst part of being a warrior, and it becomes war's lifelong repercussion. Along with memories of the person, and perhaps the way he lost his life, comes a guilty feeling that you were fortunate to survive while some of your brothers paid the ultimate sacrifice. We all had the same goal—return to the world alive. The Vietnam Memorial in Washington, DC—a.k.a. the Wall—and social media make it easier to remember our brothers who did not make it back. We cannot—and will not—forget them.

6.6 Remembrance

No words can fully explain the loss of a loved one or wholly comfort the grieving. It is tragic. It is a horrific, life-long experience. For those families who have gone through this eternal hurt, I respectfully offer the following remembrance:

Remembrance of Honor

In his or her family, the fallen or amputee will always be a respected champion, as his or her pictures and awards will be passed down for generations in recognition of the family member who sacrificed life or limb for country. The family's solace is eternal, as is their remembrance—long after the sadness and after immediate relatives have departed, he or she will endure as the family dynasty's brave hero.

Thank you, families, for your sacrifice to country!

6.7 Brothers, Where Art Thou?

It took me forty-four years to choose to write this book and even longer to begin contacting some of my Vietnam brothers. Here are some brief synopses of their lives after Vietnam:

Lance Corporal Les Fitzgerald. Fitz left the Marine Corps as a sergeant after four years of active service. He retired from the logging industry and then as manager of an asphalt plant in Washington State. When he is not off in the wilderness hunting and fishing, he and his wife, Mary, enjoy their country homestead, gardening, and relaxing with their dog and cats. They have three sons and two daughters with seven grandchildren and two great-grandchildren.

First Lieutenant Perra. Paul spent ten months in naval hospitals recovering from his wounds from the booby trap as surgeons miraculously saved his badly damaged legs and right arm, performing five major operations. During the following years, doctors, Paul, and Paul's wife, Laura, removed shrapnel that surfaced from over one hundred isolated wounds, and x-rays of his body still show "spots" where more pieces rest. Paul met Laura when he was a patient at the Chelsea Naval Hospital near Boston, Massachusetts. She was a Red Cross volunteer at the hospital. They have one daughter and two grandchildren. Paul retired from a long career as a fisheries biologist.

HN James Dew. Doc left the navy in 1972 and later returned to serve four more years at the US Naval Academy in orthopedics, leaving in 1976 as an HM2 (E-5) to attend Cal State in Los Angeles. There, he studied and worked as a surgical assistant and technician at Kaiser Permanente in West Los Angeles and Lancaster, California—where he retired after thirty-eight years. Doc now lives in South Carolina and has one son and three grandchildren.

Corporal Stevens. Paul left the Marine Corps as a sergeant after four years of active service and two tours in Vietnam. In 1997 he joined the Army National Guard to once again fight for his country in the Second Gulf War, serving two tours in Iraq as an infantryman/squad leader and eventually as a combat platoon sergeant. Paul and his wife, Nancy, live in Sanford, Florida. They have five children and fourteen grandchildren.

First Lieutenant Timberlake. Sadly, Tom passed on April 13, 2010, and prior to my attempts to contact him. He retired from the Marine Corps a lieutenant colonel after thirty years of service to his country. His numerous service medals included the Purple Heart with Gold Star (for two separate occurrences). Tom and his wife, Linda, have one daughter, Meredith.

My war brothers and I agree on the following:

It was—and always will be—our honor to serve our great country.

Appendices

A.1. The Ho Chi Minh Trail, the War's Pivotal Factor

There has never been an insurgency defeated that was able to have a safe haven outside the combat zone. Never!

—General Jack Keane, retired[61]

The above quote by General Keane should be framed and placed in a well-traveled sector near the Hall of Congress. The primary factor for the Communists' success in the Vietnam War was the Ho Chi Minh Trail (a distant second to the Ho Chi Minh Trail was the Vietcong tunnel system). To win this war, the United States had to stop the North Vietnamese infiltration into South Vietnam through Laos and Cambodia. The fact that the North Vietnamese Army was allowed to make a wide trail through neighboring countries and use it as a safe haven to ship troops and supplies, including trucks and large guns, into the south—practically at will—is one of the wonders of the Vietnam War and exemplifies America's ineptness at fighting a war politically. If we wanted to stop an insurgency, shouldn't we stop it at its known source of entry? Military forces fighting the North Vietnamese Communist insurgents should have been allowed to block all of their avenues leading to South Vietnam.

The Ho Chi Minh Trail consisted of roads, paths, tunnels, waterways, and pipelines (carrying fuel) stretching through the eastern borders of Laos and Cambodia. It has been estimated that as many as twenty-thousand Communist troops per month used this pathway to travel south. Multiple military attempts to close the trail failed, and numerous bombing missions were only temporarily successful.[62]

Political interference made it illegal for the military command to attempt to block the trail with US ground troops. The two major reasons were:

1. The Geneva Accord of 1962. This was an agreement between fourteen countries, most importantly the United States, the Soviet Union, North Vietnam, Laos, Cambodia, China, and Thailand (which borders Laos and Cambodia). In general, the agreement was to preserve the neutrality of Laos. The participating countries agreed not to enter (or support) troops into Laos and to remove all troops that were presently there. The United States was directed by presidential staff members to militarily stay out of Laos—as we had agreed in the Geneva Accord of 1962. The administrations involved in honoring this decision were the administrations of John F. Kennedy, Lyndon B. Johnson, and Richard M. Nixon. North Vietnam did not honor this agreement. Their troops continued movement through Laos and Cambodia, from prior to the Geneva Accord of 1962 to the war's end in 1975.

The presidents and staff members had legitimate concerns. They were attempting to protect South Vietnam from northern insurgency without upsetting the sovereign governments of Laos and Cambodia, both of which were teetering on the edge of communism and contending with related internal struggles for political control. If communism spread into Laos and Cambodia, it could continue into Thailand. Additionally, US presidential regimes were concerned that sending combat troops into Laos might draw China into the battle.

Note: In 1962, the political climate in Laos was described as "chaos." There were five political groups vying for control, all possessing territory. This included the

Communist army (Pathēt Lao), aided by the Soviet Union, and a "neutralist" group (led by Prince Souvanna Phouma) supported by the United States.[63]

The United States was well aware that the Communists did not honor the Geneva Accords of 1962. Here is a quote made in 1971 by W. Averell Harriman, a principal negotiator of the accords for the United States and assistant secretary of state for far eastern affairs in 1962:

"We must recognize that the North Vietnamese did not keep the Laos Agreement of 1962 for a single day."[64]

2. The Church-Cooper Amendment. This was an amendment passed by Congress in 1971 prohibiting President Nixon from waging a ground war in Cambodia, later extended to include Laos and Thailand. It was the final blockade to militarily shutting down the Ho Chi Minh Trail, and it ensured an eventual Communist victory.[65]

A warrior alone may not be a fair critic of the war he or she fought in, but who is? The "experts" have written a lot on this war. Much of it is conflicting. All of it is mere conjecture, regardless of their proclaimed wisdom. Additionally, there is always a portion of the population that wants their country to be wrong, especially when on the opposing political side. Of course, it is easy to judge and blame key players after the fact, but what decisions would the critics have made if they were president during the Vietnam era? What advice would they have given their president if they were one of his advisers? If they were commanding general of the war, would they have asked for more troops, as General Westmoreland did? After traveling the Ho Chi Minh Trail in real time, along with historical studies, including the writings from the war's select group of key advisers, I offer my humble evaluation of the Vietnam War and our failure to sustain the freedom of the South Vietnamese people:

First, the “not-all-in” strategy that we adopted is why the powerful military of the Unites States of America could not prevent the tiny Indochina country of North Vietnam from eventually invading and capturing the capital of South Vietnam. Notably, we continued to honor an agreement that the enemy ignored (the Geneva Accord of 1962). I can only demean this decision by example on the lowest level, comparing it to two grade-school children saying, “You broke your promise, so I can break mine.” However, even grade-school kids would not say, “You broke your promise, so I'm keeping mine.” If we could have successfully blocked the Ho Chi Minh Trail in northern Laos, the outcome of the Vietnam War would have been historically different.

We made poor judgments, but there were no easy decisions, and there were no right decisions. In fact, there was nothing close to easy or right. Any policy decision would be fateful to people and governments of various groups in Indochina. There were potentially devastating Cold War overtones, with US nuclear missiles pointed at Russia, and Russian nuclear missiles pointed at the United States. Our leaders were concerned about the possibility that their actions could lead to worldwide annihilation. We were caught in a dilemma, with the free world (mostly defended by the United States) versus communism (Russia, China, and North Vietnam). Our strategy became to win a war without pissing Cold War adversaries off—too much—and without spreading the war into other Indochina countries (Laos, Cambodia, and Thailand).

Note: On September 18, 1964, Robert McNamara, the secretary of defense, declared, "A full-scaled nuclear exchange between the United States and the USSR would kill 100 million Americans in the first hour. It would kill an even greater number of Russians…."[66]

The second major reason for our failure to sustain the freedom of the South Vietnamese people was the political ineptitude of the people we were defending. Early on, there were times when we were not sure which government was in power and whether it was going to stay in power. Within the first ten months of the Johnson administration, six governments came and went.[67] The subversion of the Vietcong, their tunnel systems, and the fact that the South Vietnamese forces, with our assistance, could not effectively break them, shows ineptness at the very heart of the Republic of South Vietnam. It has been well documented that the will of the South to be politically free under a democracy was less than the resolve of the North to crush and then unify them under communism. This included the North's tenacity in withstanding our repeated bombings of their cities and countryside (akin to Britain's steadfastness in World War II in the wake of German bombings).

Although this list can go on, the third and final major reason for our failure to sustain the freedom of the South Vietnamese people was the American public's lack of resolve for a prolonged war. Wars normally start with the support of the majority of citizens, but as months turn into years, it reverses. Due to our lack of acceptable reasons to justify our losses, America was not supportive of this war for very long.

The United States of America was in chaos. There's no other way I can describe it. The pivotal year was 1968, starting with the Tet Offensive. American citizens were shocked at the number of battles that took place in key areas of South Vietnam, including in the capital of Saigon, when our government was reporting we had the Communist insurgency under control. It became obvious that the war was not going as well as the military and President Johnson and his administration were representing to the American public. On the 4th of April, Martin Luther King Jr. was assassinated, causing riots in most major cities and on college campuses. On the 6th of June, Robert F. Kennedy, a presidential candidate, was assassinated. By the end of the year, 16,899 Americans had lost their lives in Vietnam, an average of 325 per week, impacting most families and public high schools—if not directly, then indirectly.[68] Located downtown in the small rural village of Groveport, Ohio, my high school—with just over a hundred students per class—held daytime memorials in the gymnasium for fallen graduates. Many times, their sisters and/or brothers were in attendance. Time magazine wrote twenty years later, "1968 was a knife that severed past from future...."[69]

Exposed to the public in 1971 by Daniel Ellsberg (via the New York Times and the Washington Post), the top-secret Pentagon Papers (officially titled United States–Vietnam Relations, 1945–1967: A Study Prepared by the Department of Defense) revealed that many key planners of our strategies in Vietnam, including past presidents, had, for political purposes, misled the American people about US involvement and battle achievements.[70] As the press published key parts of its contents (there were more than seven-thousand pages), the American public became aware of untruths that political leaders had conveyed to them. Our soldiers were risking their lives because they thought it was the right thing to do, while politicians were rationalizing that it was the right political thing to do, especially to prevent national humiliation that a withdrawal of troops would have presented. Our leaders in Washington D.C. continued to take our youth's unlived days, acknowledging early in the war (per excerpts in the Pentagon Papers) that our military tactics may not be on a winnable course. The Pentagon Papers exposed the course President Johnson, with the support of many of his influential advisers, continually decided to take—including escalating the war incrementally by increasing the number of US troops, with subsequent deaths and injuries. The Pentagon Papers became the opposition's defining impetus, as large sectors of the American public could no longer support our involvement in Vietnam. More members of the press openly joined war critics with harsh antagonism, and many members of Congress found condemnation of the war politically beneficial. Our original conclusion for military intervention in Vietnam led Robert McNamara to later write that this decision, ultimately, "polarized America like nothing since the Civil War."[71]

Notes: The Tet Offensive (January 1968) was a series of surprise attacks by the Communists on more than one hundred South Vietnamese cities and military outposts. The US and South Vietnamese forces eventually maintained or recaptured all areas of battle, causing heavy casualties, especially on the Communist side. However, the American public, sparked by negative press coverage, began to turn against the war in masses.[72] The surprise Tet Offensive in 1968 would not have been possible had we thwarted the enemy's free passage down the Ho Chi Minh Trail.

The Pentagon Papers, completed in January 1969, revealed that major presidential cabinet members and advisers believed that the war was unwinnable, but the United States continued military operations for four more years, resulting in more than twenty-one thousand American fatalities.

The numerous other reasons for our failure to sustain freedom for the South Vietnamese people are "honorable mentions" to the three accentuated ones above. The following two shameful decisions by our leaders are examples:

1. Our military's dilution by the 354,000 substandard troops—as part of McNamara's program—was a deadly decision for multitudes of warriors, but battle success was not primary from late 1969 through 1973, when this program began to fully impact our abilities to perform effectively. It does exemplify our government's lack of commitment toward the war effort.
2. The decision of the top military brass to rotate junior officers in and out of combat every six months demonstrated a serious lack of moral commitment to the troops. The decision certainly cost a lot more lives, but we still won most battles. It does exemplify our military's lack of commitment toward the war effort.

It should also be noted that, although there is plenty of blame to go around, many individual names are excluded from this list of reasons for our failure to sustain the freedom of the South Vietnamese people. Four presidents, along with their administrations, were involved in decisions affecting this war: Eisenhower, Kennedy, Johnson, and Nixon. The later three, Kennedy, Johnson, and Nixon, were unable (or unwilling) to break the Geneva Accord of 1962 and militarily block the Ho Chi Minh Trail in Laos.

Allowing our enemy safe passage into South Vietnam—to later meet them on the battlefields—underscores our failed strategy of "not all in." It compares to a football game in which one team allows the opposing team free untouchable space down the left sideline to its ten-yard line. The Communist forces moving down the

Ho Chi Minh Trail through Laos and Cambodia were untouchable by US ground forces until they mounted at strategic inlets into South Vietnam. A military blockade of the trail at the 17th parallel in northern Laos would have prevented the enemy from establishing this passageway and forced them to primarily move south through the northern (rugged) parts of South Vietnam. It also would have required fewer US troops (and deaths) than trying to fight them throughout the countryside.

By preventing US ground forces in Laos to counter the enemy's movement on the Ho Chi Minh Trail, our presidential and congressional leaders allowed the North Vietnamese Army, along with supplies and big guns, to overtly move into positions of attack, which resulted in the cost of thousands of American, South Vietnamese, and other allied lives. This was especially true in the early and middle years of the war (1964–70), when young American men were cast into major battles, resulting in slaughters on both sides. These men, in a short few months, left their innocence at home and walked into hell. In spite of horrible losses, our troops—Army, Navy, Air Force, Marines, and the U.S. Coast Guard—were overwhelmingly victorious on the battlefields. The one untarnished fact of Vietnam is the valor of the soldiers who fought there.

Bizarrely (and perhaps hypocritically), we were not prohibited from bombing the Ho Chi Minh Trail in Laos and Cambodia (bombing Laos and Cambodia was not specifically forbidden by the Geneva Accord of 1962 as were ground troops). With one hand tied behind their backs, our military leaders used the other hand to drop 2.5 million tons of munitions on the Ho Chi Minh Trail running through Laos alone (580,000 missions), more bombs than were dropped on Europe during World War II.[73]

The bombing raids were only moderately effective. Protective bunkers, heavily-forested areas, and movements at night shielded the covert jungle trails. In addition, the enemy was fast at restoring bombed-out areas. Many bombs missed their targets. Monsoon conditions (from early May to late September) made it even more difficult to find targets through the rain, low clouds, and fog. Most of the trail could not be identified at night, causing our bombing raids to be mostly done in the daytime, as Russian-made antiaircraft guns and surface-to-air missiles took down many of our planes. The danger of being shot down surely affected pilot accuracy. Of the 766 American prisoners of war, 509 were aircrew personnel.[74] In total, over 2,400 US fixed-wing aircraft were lost over North Vietnam, Laos, and Cambodia to hostile action. Additionally, over 800 aircraft were lost to operational mishaps.[75]

If the targeting [of air power] is of good quality, then it lands on the enemy or his supplies. No good to land in the jungle, you know—nothing but monkeys and elephants.

—General Creighton William Abrams, commander of US forces in Vietnam, 1968–72[76]

In May 1967, Secretary of Defense Robert McNamara wrote in a memorandum to President Johnson, "There seems to be no sign that the bombing has reduced Hanoi's will to resist or her ability to ship the necessary supplies south. Hanoi shows no signs of ending the large war and advising the VC [Vietcong] to melt into the jungles."[77]

Notes: Laos has recently been named "The Land of a Million Bombs." Since the United States ceased bombings in 1973, thirty-four thousand people have been killed or injured by bombs that failed to detonate when we initially dropped them. Sixty percent of the victims are children. There are three-hundred additional casualties per year, with approximately 40 percent of those resulting in death.[78]

It was later revealed that we had kept two sets of books during a period of time when we were bombing the Ho Chi Minh Trail in Cambodia. Thailand prohibited air strikes into Cambodia that originated from their air base. During this period, we gave Thailand map coordinates of B-52 strikes over Vietnam and our own pilots map coordinates in Cambodia. Defense Department records indicate that approximately 3,000 combat soldiers were flown outside the authorized boundary.[79]

A.2. The Domino Theory

The domino theory, first mentioned by President Dwight D. Eisenhower in 1954, suggests that if we allow one Southeast Asian country to fall to the Communists, it could create a domino effect involving its neighbors. It was the main reason given by politicians for fighting the Communists who were attempting to conquer South Vietnam. I remember this being mentioned both in high school and boot camp, along with the belief that eventually the United States would be surrounded by communism. It had already spread to Cuba and Latin America (Guatemala).

Arguably, the domino theory—as it pertained to Southeast Asia—was later proven to be true. After South Vietnam fell to the Communists in 1975, Cambodia and Laos followed. In Cambodia, the evil Pol Pot, leader of the Communist Khmer Rouge regime, killed 1.8 million Cambodians, mostly by mass executions and sickness brought on by starvation. Members of the Khmer Rouge Communists were some of the most ruthless humans in modern times.[80]

To spare you is no profit; to destroy you is no loss.

—Kang Kek Lew, mid-level leader of the Khmer Rouge regime[81]

In Laos, several hundred-thousand Laotian citizens were killed, including over a hundred-thousand Hmong people who supported and fought for the United States during the Vietnam War. The blood-thirsty Pathēt Lao Communists identified the Hmong as having aided the United States during the war and used chemical warfare as one means to commit genocide against the Hmong villages.[82]

The United States, in humane efforts with other nations, were successful at rescuing many South Vietnamese citizens prior to its country's collapse in 1975, and Cambodian and Lao citizens prior to and during their collapse, as well as from subsequent refugee camps—primarily in Thailand. However, our political atmosphere after the US withdrawal in 1973 and South Vietnam's loss in 1975 prohibited the United States from offering in-country economic and military aid, including assistance to halt the horrific killings being conducted. The following appalling quote rationalizes America's indifference toward the Indochina genocides:

The Oriental doesn't put the same high price on life, as does a Westerner. Life is plentiful, life is cheap in the Orient.

—General William Westmoreland, commander of US forces in Vietnam 1964–68[83]

General Westmoreland's words partially explain America's ignorance of the people we were fighting. It is a common fact that the more knowledge a person has, the better his or her decisions are. In his book *In Retrospect*, Robert McNamara admitted that the Kennedy and Johnson administrations lacked high-level ethnic Southeast Asian advisers.[84] Unbeknownst to us, Asian governments operate independently from others.

They will not feel "occupied" by anyone, including larger Communist countries. Although it was a collective effort, communism in Southeast Asia was not the collaborative threat our leaders assumed it was. With this knowledge, we might not have gotten militarily involved. Some dominoes fell in Indonesia, but communism as a way of government was not a danger to the United States as a result.

A.3. Losers and Winners

Losers:

- The government of South Vietnam
- The government of Cambodia
- The government of Laos
- The people of South Vietnam, Cambodia, and Laos who experienced the horrific and inhumane side of war conducted in their homelands
- The survivors of South Vietnam, Cambodia, and Laos who—after their respective wars—lived under communism
- The surviving soldiers, US loyalists, police officers, their families, and all others in South Vietnam, Cambodia, and Laos who were killed or imprisoned by the Communists for being allies of the United States of America after their respective wars ended

The United States was not a loser (militarily). Our brave American soldiers departed Vietnam in March 1973 having won nearly all major battles and left the Vietcong and North Vietnamese armies restricted and weakened. South Vietnam fell twenty-five months later.

Winners:

- North Vietnam
- Russia
- China
- The Khmer Rouge Communists in Cambodia
- The Pathēt Lao Communists in Laos

The United States was not a winner. Leaving a fight while winning is not the same as leaving a winner.

A.4. The Never-Again Club

When it comes to the use of force, the United States should either bite the bullet or duck, but not nibble.

—General David Petraeus[85]

The "Never-Again Club" references an illusory desire to not enter wars without *full intentions* of winning and comes from a comment made by General Mark Clark in 1954 that "never-again should we be mouse-trapped into fighting another defensive war on the [Korean] peninsula." It was later expanded to include Southeast Asia.[86]

Defensive wars do not make a lot of sense. They are especially irresponsible if we allow tyrants or tyrant regimes to stay in power, as in North Korea and the evil Kim dynasty (currently Kim Jong Un) or the first Gulf War with Saddam Hussein. Ho Chi Minh, the Communist Party leader in North Vietnam during the war, would not fit a "tyrant" category. However, Pol Pot and the Khmer Rouge regime in Cambodia, along with the Pathēt Lao Communists who slaughtered US sympathizers in Laos, were arguably enabled by our failed strategy in Vietnam. After we left Vietnam, we ignored these tyrant-led atrocities that were partially created by our involvement in Vietnam and the subsequent hate of Americans by many Southeast Asian people. It would be easy to contend that we did not stop a tyrant regime, since there were none to stop in Vietnam, but that we helped create two of them. We ought not escalate war in a foreign country and—prior to its end—sign a piece of paper and scoot.

Even afterthought produces no definitive solution to preventing Communist aggression and permanently sustaining South Vietnam, Laos, and Cambodian independence a half century ago. The moral purpose for our participation has been a debate in all our foreign wars, including the two world wars. The many factors affecting geopolitical decisions at the time steered our gradual involvement and buildup of troops in South Vietnam and then its reverse. Many of these factors have not been included in this brief summary, for two reasons: first, this is a brief summary and is not intended to include the countless incidental factors influencing our political and military actions at the time; and second, the lack of abundant study on many of these influences prohibits me from reaching a confident opinion. The only "confident" conclusion is that our half-assed intervention was a mistake from the beginning. The second-guessing of decisions and the placing of individual blame on historical figures by the "experts" on Vietnam have turned out numerous conflicting assessments that I have no wish to augment.

The legacy of Vietnam is that of a war started for political motives and run unsuccessfully by politicians. Although all the human and financial costs of this relatively small war cannot be listed, here are a few bullet points:[87]

- 58,200-plus Americans who died
- 10,000-plus American amputees
- 2,400-plus POWs and MIAs
- 250,000-plus vets suffering from PTSD and other illnesses related to service in Vietnam
- Financial costs of the war (United States): More than $168 million
- Ongoing financial costs (including veteran compensations): More than $500 billion
- South Vietnamese military deaths: 200,000–250,000

- 5,000-plus allied military deaths (South Korea, Australia, Thailand, Philippines, New Zealand)
- One million North Vietnamese Communist deaths
- Inhumane costs:
  - Two million civilian deaths on all sides in Vietnam during the war
  - Two million civilian and military deaths in Cambodia from Pol Pot's Khmer Rouge regime's takeover and genocide
  - 200,000-plus civilian and military deaths from the Communist takeover in Laos, mostly from war crimes
  - More than 34,000 civilian deaths and injuries (especially from bombs) after the wars in Vietnam, Laos, and Cambodia
  - Agent Orange aftereffects—all sides, including American veterans and their offspring who have suffered birth defects

The twentieth century was the bloodiest in human history, with more than 160 million killed in wars. This incredible number breaks down to 4,383 lives per day.[88] Barbara W. Tuchman's Pulitzer Prize–winning novel, *The Guns of August*, details one month at the start of World War I.[89] Since Vietnam was never a "declared war" and we used an incremental approach regarding policies and troop strength, there is not an impactful starting month that could be compared to August 1914. There were no major events that began our involvement. Our "guns of August" started during the Eisenhower administration and stretched to the Kennedy administration and through the Johnson and Nixon years in office. Our leaders could never acceptably answer the oft-asked question, "Why are we in Vietnam?" In World War I, our ancestors were fighting a "war to end all wars." The Vietnam War had no defining purpose that could be supported and sustained by the American public. We were there to stop the spread of communism in faraway lands, but that reasoning was not enough to satisfy the American public's waning appetite for war. South Vietnam was not an American ally in the sense that Great Britain and France were in the world wars. Additionally, our attempt to fight the Vietnam War by way of a proxy approach was doomed from the start, which ultimately empowered antiwar sentiment. Similar to a board game, we combatants were toy soldiers being navigated by dice-tossing Cold War superpowers—the United States and Russia—with the possibility that the loser would overturn the table and throw the pieces at the winner. If that sounds a little over the top, consider this: in 1960, at the United Nations General Assembly, Nikita Khrushchev, the man who had replaced Joseph Stalin as Premier of the Soviet Union, banged his shoe on the table in anger.[90] Contrary to the war-to-end-all-wars, the Vietnam War could have been the war to end humanity. We were setting a fuse that could have ignited a nuclear holocaust if lit. Major wars have started for lesser reasons than this. We were fortunate that the temperamental leader of Russia—in a craze—did not scream, "*Nuke 'em!*"

Bombs do not choose, they will hit everything.
—Nikita Khrushchev[91]

Many Americans were more than just concerned that Khrushchev would start a nuclear war. They built thousands of underground backyard bomb shelters during the 1950s and early '60s. There are no accurate records of how many because families kept them secret in order to conceal them from neighbors and even relatives who would come knocking if there was a nuclear disaster. They were built with space and supplies for the immediate family only. Many were built in the middle of the night. One public opinion poll in the early '60s showed that 40 percent of Americans had a fallout shelter or were considering building one.[92] During my grade-school years at Brice Elementary School in Brice, Ohio, we partook in drills in which we each hid under our desks in case Russia dropped an atomic bomb nearby.

In 1965, Barry McGuire recorded a Vietnam protest song titled "Eve of Destruction" (written by P. F. Sloan), which swiftly became a hit and included the following lyrics:[93]

If the button is pushed, there's no running away
There'll be no one to save with the world in a grave
Take a look around you, boy, it's bound to scare you, boy
But you tell me over and over and over again my friend
Ah, you don't believe we're on the eve of destruction

Did America learn a political lesson from Vietnam? The short answer is no, but which previous wars did we learn lessons from? The Never-Again Club does not denounce war, but it decries the defensive way we fought the Korean War. Our strategy in Vietnam repeated the Korean War philosophy of counterinsurgency that General Clark warned about in his "never again" statement. Contrarily, the "Again Club" surfaced (again) in the Gulf War (Operation Desert Storm, 1991), allowing Saddam Hussein to stay in power, necessitating a second gulf war (Iraq War, 2003–11).

Lessons from war are defined by historians and interpreted by politicians. Both of these sources can be biased and thus inaccurate. Barbara Tuchman wrote, "The lessons learned proved wrong for the next war."[94] Although Tuchman was describing an offensive way the French generals fought World War I (and subsequently World War II), her words warn against embracing policies based upon the wrong lessons.

What would our planet be like without wars? Tyrants (who would still engage in war with one another) would probably rule the world. "World peace" is an ideological pipe dream. Earthlings have been on a progressive path of self-destruction since biblical times. The saying "Freedom is not free" is true, as witnessed by the loss of uncountable brave soldiers defending America's liberty for the past two-and-a-half centuries. But are all wars necessary and worth the human and economic costs before, during, and afterward? Most of us from the baby-boomer generation would answer that our war was unnecessary, but we will soon become extinct. Our blood-splattered lessons from 'Nam will be entrusted to historians, and will become a small fragment of American antiquity. Our country's future war makers will likely not bother to over-explore or research it. If America did learn something from Vietnam, it is temporary at best.

History repeats—repeats—repeats!

There is one lesson learned and not forgotten by our adversaries that has been—and will continue to be—propagated against us as long as we are a power or a participant in future wars:

We abandon our foreign in-country supporters once we no longer need them and when it becomes politically unpopular to militarily protect them.

We did it in Vietnam, Cambodia, Laos, and Iraq (after the first Gulf War). Our political leaders stood still, refusing to militarily get involved again, while these "friends" (along with many of their families) were gassed with chemical weapons, harshly beaten, raped, imprisoned, and slaughtered by the regimes of Communist Vietnam, Pol Pot, the Pathēt Lao, and Saddam Hussein. The following quote sums the world's judgment of the US indifference to the human crimes being perpetrated upon our foreign in-country supporters during the fall of South Vietnam and Cambodia:

We listened with horror as your President said, 'We will stand by our friends, we will honor our commitments. We will uphold our country's principles.'

America is now at its nadir, but we did not realize that even with your Watergate experience you could once more plumb such depths of mendacity and such hypocrisy.[95]

—James Alexander Rentoul and Howard Norman, Oxford, England, 1975

Fighting a war is not just about winning it, unless you are one of the combatants. The events and stability afterward complete its purpose. In future wars it may be necessary that in order to gain support from our allies, an official document must be signed by the president *and* Congress asserting our firm commitment and protection to the loyal people in their respective countries afterward. One of our learned lessons from past wars should be:

Never again shall we turn our back on our friends.

A.5. My Story
by Toum Bou Kim

Author's note: The inhumanity of war suffered by noncombatants—local people and their families—is habitually eclipsed by historical statistics, irrespective of the fact that these people commonly endured more hardships than the soldiers who fought the battles. The evil Pol Pot led a genocide that killed and starved to death nearly two-million Cambodian people—more than 20 percent of the country's population. Many of their bodies were buried in mass graves in areas that became known as the "killing fields." The following is the story of Toum Bou Kim, the wife of San Kim, an honorable man whom I had the pleasure of working with after he and his wife came to America. Toum documents hers and San's plight and escape from Cambodia and the Khmer Rouge Communist regime, beginning in April 1975. It is one personal story among millions who have suffered war's untold anguish.

I was born in Phnom Penh, Cambodia, in 1949, the second of ten children born to my parents, Bou-Plouk and Okhem-Tramony. I had three brothers and six sisters. My parents were educated as teachers, and both spoke French. My father was a high-school principal and preferred that my mother not work. Instead, she remained at home to care for their children. In 1970, I graduated from high school. Afterward, through on-the-job training, I became a nurse in the infirmary PM (private and military) in Phnom Penh. Three months later, I was married to a soldier named Mao-Samoeurn. We had two children, a girl and a boy. In 1974, he died fighting the Vietnam Communists in Cambodia. When I became widowed, I had to work to take care of my daughter, aged three, and my son, aged one.

The rest of this story begins in 1975, when the Communist regime of Khmer Rouge, led by Pol Pot, entered Phnom Penh and forced all the people into the countryside. At this time, I took my children, plus some clothes and milk for my baby, and hurried to find my parents. I saw them on the street with two of my sisters, aged thirteen and eight. All they could carry was something to eat and some clothes. We were separated from another brother and sister who lived nearby; I didn't know where they had gone because the Communists were forcing everyone out of the city in many directions. They used gunfire to hurry the people to evacuate. All of the hospitals were also evacuated. Patients and beds were put out on the street, and cries of "Help!" could be heard everywhere.

Whole families of those who refused to leave were shot. When the Communist army found out who had been soldiers in the previous Lon Nol regime, they arrested and killed them. Announcements were made over the radio with instructions regarding where to go and what to take. The road was filled with thousands of people. We walked during the day, and at night we slept in the fields. Often it rained. After the Communist army got the people out of Phnom Penh, they destroyed everything left behind in our houses and apartments. They forced those who had money to give it to them and said that under this Communist regime, there was no need for money. There were no markets, no cinemas, and no restaurants.

In addition to killing enemy soldiers from the Lon Nol regime, the Communist army also killed engineers, doctors, teachers, musicians, and other professionals—mostly men. Thousands of women were left widowed, and if the Communists learned which women had been soldiers' wives, they also were killed along with their children, including babies.

After a few days, when our people had walked about one-hundred kilometers, we arrived in a small village that had been evacuated by the residents. My mother was very sick, having eaten nothing and having drunk only water. She died a few days later. My father, two sisters, and I wept over her death. I went to tell someone in the Communist army what had happened. One of the soldiers said to me, "Don't cry about your mother. She has no problems anymore." He took my mother's body and buried her. My family felt very sad, especially because there was no ceremony.

My little son's crying also made me sad because there was no milk for him. I went into the village and exchanged my new clothes for some sugar. As I was returning, I met a Communist guard who asked where I was coming from. I replied that I had been to the village to get sugar for my son. He then asked where my husband was. I answered that he had died a year ago. The guard asked if my husband had been a soldier. I lied and said, "No, a salesman."

He didn't believe me. "You look like a lady," he said and accused me of being the commander's wife. I insisted that I was not. As he looked me up and down, I began to tremble because I was so afraid he would shoot me. After he had stared at me awhile, he took a paper from his pocket, handed it to me, and ordered me to read it.

By now, I thought he had guessed that I was a teacher or a nurse. I tricked him by holding the paper upside down and saying, "I can't read; I don't know how."

After a few minutes, he said, "Go."

I quickly ran back to my family. I boiled some water with sugar and gave my son a bottle. Five days later the Communists forced everyone to move out of the village. Again, all our people walked during the daylight and slept outside at night.

After three days, my little son became very sick. There was no more sugar water available for him to drink, so I gave him thin soup made of rice and a little salt. His legs swelled as he grew worse. One night he seemed very, very sick and didn't say anything. He slept without moving, was feverish, and was breathing very fast. I watched over him all night, as I didn't know what else to do, and at six o'clock in the morning he died.

When it was time for us to start walking again, I was still weeping for my son, who had died from starvation. One of the Communist soldiers took him away to be buried, just as my mother had been. My father and sisters were very sad; they kept walking—saying nothing. I shed many, many tears as I walked, longing for my baby, whom I had held in my arms the night before but who now was sleeping in the ground like my mother. Even now, when I remember that time, many tears come to my eyes.

My family and all other people walked for many long days and finally arrived near the bank of a river named Prek Pav, a branch of the Mekong River. Since they couldn't walk any farther, the Communist army told them to remain there. Every family found something to use to build a shelter. At night, the Communists required everyone to attend a meeting about the Communist regime. One of their leaders stood up and spoke while the people sat on the ground and listened. He said that under this Communist regime, everyone must work on the farms to provide food. No one could work for his own food, and the work must begin the following day. Forty grams of rice would be distributed to the people who could work, and to those unable to work, only twenty grams plus salt.

In my family, only my thirteen-year-old sister and I were able to work. My father, my youngest sister, and my little daughter (three years old) could not. Therefore, there was not enough rice to cook. Instead, we made rice soup.

My teenage sister went to work by bus because it was so far away. Every morning at six o'clock, one of the Communists rang a bell to notify the people it was time to go to work. Some carried knives, and others carried axes for cutting down trees and preparing the ground to plant corn. While I went to work, my eight-year-old sister cooked rice soup at home. She had found wood and water for cooking, as well as some vegetables in the forest nearby. My father was not well and therefore took care of my little daughter.

My father's health grew worse, and his legs swelled due to lack of food. Many other people became sick and swollen because they were eating only rice and salt. They badly needed meat and fish. My little daughter was so hungry that she ate anything she could find from the bushes, after which she became very sick with bloody diarrhea. She was weak, and there was no medicine for her. One morning at 9:00, she died. Two men helped me make a wooden box for my daughter's body so we could bury her.

I couldn't sleep that night. I remembered the night before when my daughter had talked a lot with me. She had asked when we could go back home and had added that she was hungry and wanted some cake and sweets to eat. When I answered, "I don't know," she had cried. So I had promised, "Tomorrow we will go home." I had also told her that Mommy would buy her cakes and sweets and everything she wanted. She seemed happy after that and inquired about her brother and other things. I had wondered why she talked with me so much that night. I realized she was sick and very weak, but I didn't know we were talking for the last time.

My father heard me weeping and said, "Dear daughter, you must go to sleep. Don't be sad anymore. I know how miserable you are, but tomorrow you must go back to work. I'm worried that you will become sick."

I listened to him and said, "Yes, Daddy, I know." I loved my father very much and tried to always obey him. When I returned from work each day, I always went to my daughter's grave.

We stayed in our current location for two months. One afternoon, while the people were working, one of the Communist soldiers yelled, "Stop work!" and told us to get ready to move to Battambang. We were to leave the same night for a port where ships were waiting for us.

We left at six o'clock in the evening. A large crowd of people walked along the road. My father walked very slowly with the help of a walking stick. One kilometer down the road, I saw a family that had put things into a broken-down car and was pushing it. I asked if I might put my father in this car because his legs were swollen, and he was no longer able to walk. He looked at my father and readily agreed. Both my sisters and I helped push.

Our people walked all night long and became very sleepy. No one slept, however, because the Communists were forcing everyone to hurry to the port. Our family arrived at two o'clock in the morning, and I found a place for us to sleep. We spent a day and a night aboard a ship and arrived at the port of Kampong Chhnang at ten o'clock in the morning.

At about five o'clock the same day, we boarded a bus and rode through the provincial capitals of Kampong Chhnang and Pursat to the railroad station in Pursat, where we boarded the train to Battambang. This was a very long trip lasting two days and nights. The train stopped at a railroad station called Tepathey near a small village called Phoum Tepathey in the *srok* (group of villages) called Kas Kralor, a part of the provincial capital, Battambang. The Communists moved us off the train at five o'clock in the evening, and we were told to remain in the village overnight. The next day, we would go to the mountain called Kas Kralor, about fifteen kilometers away.

We went into the village, and I asked a family if I might use their porch for us to rest. I cooked rice for supper. While we were eating, a woman from the family whose porch we were using gave me a bowl of soup with vegetables because she saw we had only rice and salt to eat. She asked many questions about where I had come from and about our trip. As we were ready to leave early the next morning, I said goodbye to the kind woman and her family. At this moment she said, "Stop! Don't go. I will talk to my son-in-law, who is the team foreman here. I like your family and am worried about your father's swollen legs. No one has lived in Kas Kralor for a long time because of malaria." After talking to her son-in-law, she walked toward me. "He agrees," she said, "but he must first inform the village leader. You must wait for him." She added that my family could stay in her son's cottage because he was at the farm where he worked.

During the morning, I noticed a man walking toward us wearing very dirty black clothes, as if he were just coming from work, and a little girl about three years old was running to him. He picked her up in his arms and walked toward the cottage we were in. I asked if this was his cottage, and he nodded. I told him that his mother said we could stay there. He agreed that it would be okay. His mother had told him about it, and he would not be staying there but would come home every two or three days to visit his daughter. She lived with his mother-in-law because his wife had died five months ago. He came into the cottage to remove his belongings and went back to work. His name was San Kim, and his daughter was Sarom.

Later, when I was cooking rice, San Kim's mother came to tell me that the village leader had refused to allow me to stay. He had said that the *angkar* (organization in power) didn't allow people from Phnom Penh to live there and that we must leave by tomorrow. Under the Communist regime, each village had a leader, two elders (assistants), a foreman, and a team leader.

That afternoon, three men came into San Kim's cottage and told my sisters and me to leave while they talked with my father. After they left, he told me that the village foreman and two assistants had an idea: if I were to marry San Kim, my family and I could live there. If I said no, we must leave the next morning.

That night, my father and I discussed it. He said that he knew that many men in the past had wanted to marry me after I became widowed. I had said no to all of them, but this time he advised me to say yes.

"We are in the Communist regime, and life is very difficult for us. Remember that your mother and your two children have died because of it," he told me.

That night I couldn't sleep because I was thinking about my decision. I didn't know what type of man San Kim was. He had always lived in the country, and I had always lived in the capital city. However, if I said no, I didn't know what the future would be. My father was old and sick, and my two sisters were young girls. They had never known hardships such as we were experiencing. This was a difficult choice. What should I do? I finally decided to say yes, out of love for my father and sisters.

At eight o'clock the next morning, I gave my answer to the foreman, who said, "Good. You will become part of the family, and you can all live here." He then went to tell San Kim, who was at work on the farm and didn't yet know about it.

That afternoon San Kim's parents came to talk with my father about our marriage. The marriage was to be kept secret from the angkar. In the Pol Pot regime, those wishing to marry had to apply to the angkar for permission, and twenty to thirty couples were married at once in the evening, after work, to save time. At these ceremonies, the parents were called together to sit on the ground and watch. The brides and bridegrooms sat opposite each other on two long benches. A man from the angkar stood and talked about proper behavior after marriage; the couples must be honest, and they should be willing to work hard to obtain lots of rice and food for the regime. Then he told the couples to stand and hold hands. Everyone repeated, "I will" in unison. Everyone then went home. It was all very easy and the strangest ceremony I had ever seen.

There were other types of marriages as well. In some places the terrible angkar selected the prettiest young girls and forced them to marry Communist soldiers. Several of these soldiers were blind in one eye or had lost a limb in battle. Some of the young girls committed suicide. The angkar had the power to do anything without a word of protest from anyone.

At our private wedding, my father and sisters ate a lot of food since they had not had meat to eat in a long time. I ate very little because I was upset and nervous. San Kim's parents had six children. He was the oldest of four boys and two girls.

The day after I was married, a woman team leader told me, "Today you must make all your clothes black, and tomorrow you must go to work with us." In the Communist regime, everyone wore black. No color was allowed except for pieces of cotton cloth called *krama* (a scarf), which were very colorful. These were used for covering one's head to keep off the sun while working in the rice fields and for carrying home vegetables, snails, crabs, and so on. When I went to work, I wore a red krama given to me by San Kim along with a black shirt and pants. The men often wore krama tied around their waists.

My father and little sister couldn't work, so they stayed home and cooked rice. San and his older sister worked all day and came home at six o'clock. My work was near the village, and I came home at five o'clock. I never understood the methods of working on a farm. When I did something wrong, the other women laughed at me, and some said unpleasant things. I began to question San about methods used on the farm. He taught me the proper way to do things, and I practiced them using grass. One day when I was working, the women were surprised when they saw that I could work as well as they did. It was still difficult for me to do this work and get wet all the time.

Housework was not difficult because San helped me with everything. After he came home in the evening, he brought wood from the forest for cooking rice and vegetables and sometimes crabs, frogs, or fish that he caught. He fetched water home for my bath and made medicine from the bark of trees to treat my father's swelling legs. I had faith that San would be a good husband. After the first month, the swelling in my father's legs had disappeared, and he felt well. San loved me very much, as did my mother-in-law. She helped me with anything I did not know how to do.

In the summertime, when the rainy season stopped, the fields grew dry and the farmers could harvest the rice. During this time, the leader of the women's team told all the childless women to get some clothes ready—plus something to sleep on—because they would be working far away and would have to sleep at the work site. I didn't see my family and San for almost three months, until the rice harvesting was over. The angkar then told the leaders that the childless women must join other single adults to help build a dam. San, my teenage sister, and I went far away to work on the dam.

In the Communist regime, we harvested rice twice per year. At that time, the angkar said that the distribution of rice to each family must be stopped. He ordered the village leader to build a large kitchen. The rations were three large spoonfuls of rice for adults, two large spoonfuls for children who could work, and one for small children who could not work.

The entire family had to work, with the exception of babies. The older men were made leaders of children aged five to nine, who were given the job of collecting cattle dung to be used as fuel and fertilizer. Elderly women were babysitters.

The angkar said that those who didn't work would receive only one large spoonful of rice, as if they were babies. The rice portion for those who were sick and didn't work for three days was reduced to one large spoonful. The sick had no doctor, no medicine, and reduced rice portions. Many people who got sick died.

In 1976, the Communist army brought three thousand people from the province of Takeo to live in our group of villages. Five hundred newcomers came into our village to live. There was not enough rice to go around, so the angkar told the kitchen leader to prepare and distribute rice soup instead of rice.

I was four-months pregnant and became extremely tired. I felt unable to carry the heavy loads of earth (for building a dam), yet I was required to work all day and also at night, from 7:00 a.m. to 10:00 p.m. San begged the women's team leader to allow me to return to a job in the village. As a result, she assigned me to light work in the kitchen, where I washed a lot of dishes and swept the floors.

A month later, San and the other men returned to plow the farm again. He worked near the mountain, Tathoc, and came home each evening. My teenage sister worked at the same place but had to remain there overnight. During this time, my father became sick with fever, chills, and swollen legs because he ate nothing but soupy rice. He didn't work for two weeks. After his fever left, he was very hungry, but I had nothing for him to eat. San was very busy at work during the day, but after work he always left a bamboo fishing trap in the Timberlake. Each morning my little sister went to pick it up. Some days there were fish, crabs, or frogs, and some days there was nothing.

When I was eight months pregnant, my father became seriously ill. His whole body was swollen. One evening he seemed especially weak and tired and told me he was hungry for some cooked rice and potato. I told him not to worry, that tomorrow I would try to beg some extra rice from the kitchen leader and cook it for him. San said that he would find some potatoes for him on the mountain the next day. My little sister added that she would pick up the fishing trap, and if she found any fish in it, she'd cook it for him. Hearing all this made my father happy, and he looked forward to having more to eat the next day.

As promised, my sister went to pick up the fishing trap the following day, and I went to beg for rice. San went to work as usual. The woman kitchen leader gave me very little cooked rice—only three small spoonfuls. My sister found two crabs and one fish in the trap. She told me, "One fish for father, and two crabs for us." After I cooked everything, I called my father to eat, but he didn't answer. It was then that I noticed his head had fallen down on his pillow. I cried and hugged his body, and my little sister ran crying to tell the foreman. Two men soon came with something for carrying my father's body. They buried him about thirty meters behind our house under a large tree. I wanted so much to tell San and my teenage sister about my father's death, but they were too far away. He had died of starvation and lack of medicine, as did my mother and two children.

That evening, I saw San coming home with some potatoes. As soon as he handed them to me, I began to cry. I shed many tears because everything my father wanted to eat had come too late for him. When I told San, he was shocked and immediately ran to look at his grave. I know he felt very sad. He had not been there to be with me before the burial.

San left for work the next morning, and I asked him to tell my teenage sister what had happened. She came home about three o'clock that afternoon. We cried together as we went over to the bough under which my father was buried. She said she had not seen him for eight long months and had missed him so very much. The group leader would not allow her to come home until after he died. The following morning, my sister returned to work.

My baby son was born on December 10, 1976. At this time, there was more rice coming from the farm, and the angkar told the kitchen leader to distribute cooked rice instead of soup. I decided to name our baby Virsna, which means fat or lucky, because when he was born, we had more rice to eat.

San no longer worked on the farm but was a fisherman. All fishermen worked in pairs. Every day, they caught fish for the kitchen, but San sometimes hid a fish in his shirt or karma for our family.

Two weeks later, sixteen Khmer Rouge families traveled into our area by oxcart. Four families were assigned to our village to replace the previous leaders. The four men were appointed as the leader, two assistants, and a foreman. The women would act as two kitchen leaders and two team leaders. The new leaders told us that there would be a meeting every night after dinner. They said that we must be willing to work hard and refrain from stealing anything, that we were not allowed to have pots and pans and must bring them all to the kitchen, and that we must not take food home except for those who were too sick to walk. The leaders told the people to build a hospital for those who were sick more than three days. They said that sick people didn't eat very much and therefore only one large spoonful of rice was to be given to each patient at the hospital. At night we were to sleep. We must not walk from one place to another and must not talk or discuss anything amongst ourselves. Every night they met with us and repeated these demands.

When Virsna was twenty days old, a Khmer Rouge woman leader told me to work in the garden to pull weeds and plant vegetables for the kitchen. Before work, I took my baby to my mother-in-law. At work, I met three older women and a young woman about eight-months pregnant who was a newcomer from the province capital, Takeo. I learned that her husband was a soldier who had been killed by the Communist army five months before she had come there. Her name was Saroeurn, and we became close friends.

A month later, the angkar told all leaders to build a long house near the mountain Tepathey and to gather all children between eight and twelve to live in it. My little sister, now almost nine, was taken to live and work there. Many of the children were crying because of the separation from their parents. My little sister was very sad and didn't want to go. I helped her get her clothes ready and told her not to worry. "It isn't too far, dear sister, and you can still come to see me." I loved her very much, of course, but realized that it was necessary.

Two months later, in 1977, a new order came from the angkar. All kitchen leaders were told that only the people who worked far away were allowed to have cooked rice. Those who worked near the village were given soupy rice because there was not enough to go around. I worked in the village and was allowed only three large spoonfuls of soupy rice. It wasn't enough because I was nursing our baby, but San always kept some of his cooked rice for me when he came home from fishing. My little sister also brought me some of her rice at noon and sometimes in the evening. I always kept some fish and vegetables for her that San found in the fields. My friend Saroeurn was as hungry as I was, for she had a baby girl almost two months old. Sometimes when I had rice and fish from San and my sister, I shared it with her. She was always very grateful.

During this time, everyone was very hungry and was always looking for food. After work, some found small frogs, crabs, and snails on the farms and vegetables in the fields. Some ate snakes, rats, lizards, and insects. Others stole sweet potatoes and corn from the farms. When the Communist army saw people stealing, they shot them on the spot. Everyone was very thin from working hard and not having enough food. This was not true with the Khmer Rouge families. They were all fat. They ate cooked rice, had enough food, and didn't work very hard. Sometimes they would kill a cow to serve at a party for themselves.

Later in 1977, San's brother married a young girl nearby in a ceremony for twenty-two couples performed by the angkar. The village leader liked San's brother very much and allowed him and his bride to live with them in their large house. After this, San no longer worked as a fisherman. The village leader, with whom San's brother lived, wished to have San as his assistant to cut bamboo, which was used to make tools and utensils. San did not want to be separated from me because he worried that I would be alone with our baby and not have enough to eat, but anyone needed by the angkar had to go without protest. While San was gone, I lived in our cottage with little Virsna and without any extra food. After two weeks, San was missing Virsna and me and worried about us. He had captured a rabbit, which he cured with salt and hung in the sun to dry, along with a wood potato and a snake. The leader, however, refused to allow him to come home. That night he didn't tie up his oxen because he wanted them to wander back to our village. The oxen always knew where they lived. The next morning, he asked the leader if he could look for his "lost" oxen, and the leader agreed. San quickly took another oxcart to ride home, traveled all day, and arrived at six o'clock in the evening. What a happy face! He brought many kinds of food to last us a long time. I shared some of this food with his daughter, Sarom, who lived nearby with her grandmother, and saved some for my little sister. The following morning San found his oxen grazing in a field about fifty meters from our house. After lunch, he tied the oxen to the oxcart and returned to the forest.

Virsna was not yet a year old and received only one large spoonful of soupy rice per day, although I was still nursing him. I was assigned to fetch water and put it on the garden each day. It was extremely heavy work, and it made me sick because I was not strong enough to carry water in two large pails on poles over my shoulders thirty times a day. After I stayed home for three days from exhaustion, a team leader told me I must go to the hospital. I took Virsna with me plus a few possessions. There were many patients in the hospital—some with fever and chills, some who were swollen, and some women who had just given birth. I saw many little girls, about ten or eleven years old, who were "nurses" and a young girl about fourteen years old who was a "doctor." They were the children of Khmer Rouge people. When I came in as a new patient, they searched my bag and removed my album of family pictures that I had carefully kept for a long time. They were photos of my family during the Lon Nol regime. They also took my watch and some broken jewelry. They said, "Beware! You are not allowed to keep anything from the Lon Nol regime." I was told to sleep on a small bamboo cot.

Good medicine was provided for the Khmer Rouge families, but the medicine for others was worthless for treating sick patients. It sometimes made them even sicker, and I always threw mine away.

I stayed in the hospital to rest and patiently accepted the ration of one large spoonful of rice without complaining. Five days later I saw my friend Saroeurn and her baby. She was as sick as I was and took the bed next to mine. Saroeurn knew how to knit a hat and socks for her baby, and the nurses enjoyed watching her. They had never seen knitting before. Everyone began to look for wool to give to Saroeurn to make sweaters, hats, and scarves for them. After that they gave Saroeurn extra rice (two or three more spoonfuls), which she shared with me.

At that time, the little nurses had as much power as the angkar. If they liked someone, the patient was given more rice, and they sometimes withheld rice from those they did not like. Once, when they were distributing rice, I noticed a woman patient trick them into giving her two servings. When the nurses found out, they took her rice and ruthlessly beat her on the head with a large spoon. It was a terrible thing to watch. After a month in the hospital, Saroeurn and I felt better and were discharged by a young girl "doctor." The following day a kitchen leader assigned us to the job of crushing rice near the kitchen.

One day in 1977, Communist soldiers and families who had just married from the capital province of Kampong Speu moved into our village. We found that their purpose was to live with us and spy on the Khmer Rouge families that were in charge. Our people told them about everything, including the cruelties and deaths. One of the Communist soldiers pretended to be sick and went to the hospital to observe the nurses. Later they determined that the Khmer Rouge families had not been loyal to the angkar. The soldiers arrested and killed all of them. The village leader's family was killed, but the leader, along with San's brother, escaped. The soldiers arrested San's brother's wife and took her and her three-month-old baby to a prison-like building. They beat her to learn the whereabouts of her husband. She protested that she didn't know. This was true—her husband had run away without telling her where he was going. The Communists didn't believe her and beat her into unconsciousness, and she died. One of the soldiers picked up her baby by the leg and tossed him into the air. He fell to the ground and died near his mother's body. This torture shocked all of us, including the other prisoners.

This Communist regime was really evil. Anyone who stole something was put in a prison and beaten every day until he or she finally died from wounds or starvation. If the Communist soldiers overheard people taking about their lives in the previous Lon Nol regime, they would force them to dig their own graves, beat them with a club, and then bury them while they were still breathing. Others were accused of being agents of Lon Nol and were taken out to a field and shot.

After the assistant who was working with San ran away because he feared the Communists were going to kill him, San returned to the forest to cut bamboo. Three days later the Communists came to San's father's house in the middle of the night. They accused him of telling his other son to run away with the assistant, and they killed San's father. The family could not save him and were afraid they would kill all of them also. San found out that his father had been killed and came home the next day. He was very sad.

The Communists also killed the doctor, all the little nurses, and the young Khmer Rouge family members who were leaders at the children's center. Afterward, they allowed all the children to return home to their parents. My little sister was released from the center, and because she missed our other sister so much, she begged me to allow her and a friend to visit her at her work location. I allowed her to go but on the condition that she not stay long. Her older sister had worked for many months with the group of single people excavating to build a dam. They were by a river named Kang Hot, near orange groves and fields of potatoes. She sent some of both back to us.

My little sister did not return for a month, and I was worried about her because after she left, the angkar told all the village people that travel to and from other places must stop. If they were seen, they would be killed. The angkar was worried about the Vietnamese Communists who were now fighting the Khmer Rouge Communists at the border of Vietnam.

I was one of fifteen men and women who were sent the next morning to work on the mountain where the forest needed to be cleared before corn was planted. San worked at plowing on the farm, and my mother-in-law took care of Virsna. My job was very tiring. Every day we went to the top of a high mountain and chopped down tall trees with a hatchet. During this time, I was sad. There was never a time or a reason to be happy. In three months, we cleared the mountain forest and planted corn. We were sent back to work on the farm harvesting rice. Meanwhile, San was plowing far away and couldn't come home.

Two months later, a woman leader in the group told all the women with babies that they must work in the village threshing rice. We all worked very hard to produce lots of rice twice a year, but the Communists still didn't give us enough to eat. The people were hungry and were tempted to steal rice. Saroeurn told me to steal some in order to help feed our families. I said that I didn't know how to steal and couldn't do it. I was afraid that I'd be killed if the Communists found out. Saroeurn said that she would steal the rice if I would cook it. Every day, she would put rice in a little cloth bag, which she hung from a long string around her neck. When the bag was full, she put it inside her blouse. The other women stole rice the same way. I was not to work one day but would stay home and cook. She would explain to the leader that I was home taking care of my sick baby. I agreed to her plan and stayed home.

On the day I stayed home, it happened that a leader informed everyone at work that they would be working far away the following day and were to take the babies with them to be watched by two older women. Afterward, he came to my house to inform me of the new plans. When the leader opened my door and came in, I was so surprised and scared that I shook all over. He had caught me in the act of cooking rice. He accused me of stealing the rice and collected it in his hands to show the village assistants. He forced Virsna and me out of the house and toward the assistants. One assistant suggested putting me in prison, and I began to cry. I thought I would die along with Virsna and that San would never know what had happened to us. One of the leaders pushed me toward the prison, but another assistant said, "Stop! Not yet! First we will punish her for a week as a lesson for the others not to steal." The punishment consisted of reducing my portion of rice by half and also forcing me to add two hours to my workday—one in the morning and one in the evening. I was hungry all the time, but on the second day, I met a man who had been with San, and he gave me a bag of potatoes that San had sent me. He knew this man was coming to see his wife who had just given birth.

My punishment lasted six days, and I was very frightened because in just one more day, the village leader was going to put me in prison. That night, around two o'clock in the morning, I heard a loud boom. The Vietnamese army had advanced near Battambang and was firing explosives. The Khmer Rouge soldiers ran to their homes to get their families and belongings. They quickly fled in oxcarts to the mountains near Thailand. They told us to collect our things and follow them. At the prison, the soldiers shot all the prisoners they were guarding before running away. I too would have been shot if I had been placed there earlier.

All the people moved out of their homes after the Khmer Rouge left but did not follow them. I saw San with a large sack of rice on his shoulders coming toward our house. He told me to get ready to leave while he went to pick up Sarom from his mother-in-law. The Khmer Rouge army came back several times as we were leaving to force us to go to the mountain where they were hiding, Trachac Chet, but the battle had begun. The North Vietnamese, who now occupied our village, demanded that we stay. Some of the Khmer Rouge families tried to mix in with us, but we identified them to the Vietnamese. The people were angry and wanted revenge against the Khmer Rouge people. They had slaughtered and starved to death many individuals in our families. Some wanted the satisfaction of killing them with their own knives, but the Vietnamese shot all of them.

For almost seven months, we had been looking for both my sisters. I had no information on them and feared the worst. The Vietnamese Communist regime was even crueler than the Khmer Rouge regime under Pol Pot. The people were suffering more hunger, violence, and death. It seemed that we would never escape the horrible life under the Communists. It didn't matter what regime moved in and took over. They were all brutal and terrible people. San and I discussed attempting to flee toward the border and into Thailand. We decided that we needed to try to protect and save our remaining family—now four of us, including Sarom and Virsna. We traveled by night and either hid during the day or mixed in with other local people at the places we stopped. After walking for six nights, we reached the Thai border.

We lived in refugee camps for nearly two years and were put on a list to be taken to America. At one of the camps, I met a friend of my little sister. She said that my teenage sister had sent her younger sister to live with a family that had lost their own children. The teenage sister was being forced by the angkar to marry a Communist soldier (she was fifteen years old at the time). She had fled to another place, but the angkar had found her—but she had escaped again and had fled toward Thailand. My little sister's friend did not have additional information on either sister.

At one of the refugee camps, I got a job working in the registration office for the Supplementary Feeding Program for Refugee Children. On April 4, 1981, we had an interview and test at the American embassy. Two weeks later we moved from Thailand to Indonesia, where we attended a program for three months to learn English. We also enrolled in a cultural-orientation-training project. During that time, I volunteered to work in the refugee community as a leader of the Khmer (Cambodian) Women's Association.

On January 13, 1982, we moved to Singapore for two days and then flew to the United States. We spent one night in California and the next morning flew from San Francisco to Columbus, Ohio. We arrived on January 16, 1982. It was very, very cold, and there was white snow everywhere—something we had not seen before. A lot of American people were at the airport to welcome us.

The first night, my children were so happy. They played all night and didn't go to sleep at all. This had been our dream: that we would safely escape from the Communist regimes and find freedom in America.

San and I love living in America and in Columbus, Ohio. We now have four children and fourteen grandchildren. We thank God daily for saving us from death and leading us to this wonderful country.

Resources

Many thanks and recognition to the following marines and naval corpsmen, who helped me remember our time in Vietnam and accurately trace events:

James Dew

Les Fitzgerald

Sam Hale

David Hansen

Steven Lepley

Paul Perra

Fred Stalzer

Paul Stevens

A special thank you to Linda Timberlake who, along with daughter Meredith, assisted with my inquiries regarding her husband, the late Lieutenant Colonel Thomas Timberlake.

A special thank you to Toum Bou Kim for the courage to share her heartbreaking story of suffering and survival while she was living under the Khmer Rouge regime in Cambodia.

An acknowledgment to the Defense POW/MIA Accounting Agency of the US government in Washington, DC.

Initial cover photo: Elite Editing

Photo editing: DODD Camera, Lewis Center, Ohio

Final book cover: Charles Nichols

Style, final copyediting and format editing: Amie Newcomb

Acknowledgments

Almost everyone needs encouragement to start a project, stay with it, and complete it. My support and encouragement, along with some very good advice and edits, came from my wife, Connie.

Thank you to my brother and sisters, who kept my letters from Vietnam for over forty years, and for their contributions from memories of the Vietnam years. I will list them by first names: Linda, Bill, Nancy, Peggy, and Patty (now deceased, but I still treasure her many heartfelt letters).

To Les Fitzgerald's contributions: he humped a radio beside me in Vietnam and became my best friend—a friendship that became latent from time and distance but did not lapse and is now as strong as ever.

Provisions

Names were used with permission from each person or family. All other names were changed ("not his real name" or "not his real nickname") to protect those not contacted or who did not reply to written requests for interaction by the author.

Exception: Lieutenant Colonel Leftwich, a brave marine who is a public figure. Appropriately, a statue of William Leftwich stands in front of the administration building at Quantico, Virginia. The visitor center is co-named in his honor at the USNA in Annapolis, Maryland; the Leftwich Trophy goes to outstanding officer leaders in his name; and the USS *Leftwich* (a destroyer) was named in his honor.[96]

The Han River is an immense waterway flowing south from the Da Nang Harbor, splitting into two rivers and later branching into multiple tributaries. The "mother river," the Han, is used in all text since the tributaries were not always identifiable or specified on our missions south of Da Nang.

AO ("area of operation") was used by most of the men and field commanders in Vietnam, signaling a specific and smaller mission as compared to *TAOR* ("tactical area of responsibility"), which included Marine territories incorporating the northern areas of South Vietnam.

References

[1] “*Combat!*”, *Wikipedia*, https://en.wikipedia.org/wiki/Combat!_(TV_series)

[2] “Capital Punishment by the U.S. Military,” *Wikipedia*, https://en.wikipedia.org/wiki/Capital_punishment_by_the_United_States_military.

[3] “Onward, Christian Soldiers,” *Wikipedia*, https://en.wikipedia.org/wiki/Onward_Christian_Soldiers.

[4] “Statistical Information about Casualties of the Vietnam War,” *National Archives*, accessed April 29, 2008, https://www.archives.gov/research/military/vietnam-war/casualty-statistics.html.

[5] “Forrest Gump,” *Wikipedia*, https://en.wikipedia.org/wiki/Forrest_Gump.

[6] “Vietnam War Casualties,” *Military Wikia*, http://military.wikia.com/wiki/Vietnam_War_casualties.

[7] “Cu Chi Tunnels Tours,” *Viator*, https://www.viator.com/Ho-Chi-Minh-City-attractions/Cu-Chi-Tunnels/d352-a1687.

[8] “Sikorsky CH-54 Skycrane,” *CombatAircraft.com*, http://combataircraft.com/en/Military-Aircraft/Sikorsky/CH-54-Skycrane/.

[9] “Kit Carson Scouts,” *VietnamWar.net*, http://www.vietnamwar.net/KitCarsonScouts.htm.

[10] Gary Roush, “Helicopter Losses during the Vietnam War,” Vietnam Helicopter Pilots Association, http://www.vhpa.org/heliloss.pdf.

[11] Ibid.

[12] Paul Torres, “‘Chosin Few’ Honored during 1st Marine Division 7th Anniversary,” Marine Corps Association & Foundation, February 2, 2011, https://www.mca-

marines.org/leatherneck/gallery/chosin-few-honored-during-1st-marine-division-70th-anniversary.

13 "Chips the War Hero Dog," *Dispatches*, February 2018, https://army.togetherweserved.com/army/newsletter2/18/newsletter.html.

14 "Vietnam," United States War Dogs Association Inc., http://www.uswardogs.org/war-dog-history/vietnam/.

15 "Purple Haze," *Wikipedia*, https://en.wikipedia.org/wiki/Purple_Haze.

16 http://military.wikia.com/wiki/Vietnam_War_casualties.

17 "The M-197 20 mm Automatic Gun," *Aircav.com*, http://www.aircav.com/cobra/m197.html.

18 Leon Watson, "Anyone for Roasted Rat? Restaurant in Vietnam Offers Rodent on a Stick," *Daily Mail*, December 4, 2013, http://www.dailymail.co.uk/news/article-2518121/Vietnam-restaurant-offers-roasted-rat-stick-local-delicacy.html#ixzz4kjRSgVtU.

19 Hamilton Gregory, *McNamara's Folly: The Use of Low-IQ Troops in Vietnam War* (West Conshohocken, PA: Infinity Publishing, 2015), xiii.

20 Ibid, xiii-xiv.

21 Ibid, 164.

22 Ibid, 196.

23 "Project 100,000: New Standards Program," RAND, accessed June 2018, http://www.rand.org/content/dam/rand/pubs/monographs/MG265/images/webG1318.pdf.

24 Gregory, 119–120.

25 Mark Depu, "Vietnam War: The Individual Rotation Policy," November 13, 2006, http://www.historynet.com/vietnam-war-the-individual-rotation-policy.htm.

26 https://en.wikipedia.org/wiki/Forrest_Gump.

27 Brad Smithfield, "'Fragging' Is the Deliberate Killing of a Senior Ranking Military Officer, Usually with a Frag

Grenade with over 700 Cases near the End of the Vietnam War," *Vintage News*, June 1, 2016, https://www.thevintagenews.com/2016/06/01/fragging-is-the-deliberate-killing-of-a-senior-ranking-military-officer-usually-with-a-frag-grenade-with-over-700-cases-near-the-end-of-the-vietnam-war-2/.

[28] Ibid.

[29] Gregory, 177.

[30] Mike Perry, "Claymore: World's Most Famous Mine?" *Special Operations*, May 15, 2014, https://specialoperations.com/28997/claymore-worlds-famous-mine/.

[31] Lawrence H. Climo, "Doctor to the Montagnards," *Vietnam*, December 1999, 49.

[32] "Command Chronology, December 1970," folder 060, US Marine Corps History Division Vietnam War Documents Collection, Vietnam Center and Archive, Texas Tech University, https://www.vietnam.ttu.edu/reports/images.php?img=/images/1201/1201021037.pdf.

[33] Herb Friedman, "Venereal Disease Propaganda," *Psywarrior.com*, http://www.psywarrior.com/PSYOPVD.html.

[34] James Dew (navy corpsman during the Vietnam War, 1970–71) in discussion with the author, November 2017.

[35] US Department of Defense, "Authorization for Disclosure of Medical or Dental Information," DD Form 2870, December 2003, http://www.esd.whs.mil/Portals/54/Documents/DD/forms/dd/dd2870.pdf.

[36] "All Quiet on the Western Front," *Wikipedia*, https://en.wikipedia.org/wiki/All_Quiet_on_the_Western_Front.

[37] https://en.wikipedia.org/wiki/Combat!_(TV_series)

[38] "Flak Jacket," *Wikipedia*, https://en.wikipedia.org/wiki/Flak_jacket.

[39] Nick Turse, "For America, Life Was Cheap in Vietnam," *New York Times*, October 9, 2013, https://www.nytimes.com/2013/10/10/opinion/for-america-life-was-cheap-in-vietnam.html.

[40] "Comparison of the AK-47 and M16," *Wikipedia*, https://en.wikipedia.org/wiki/Comparison_of_the_AK-47_and_M16.

[41] David Gerhardt's squad book, titled *Memoranda*, 1971.

[42] David Gerhardt, Communication Talks, B/S Walks: The Self-Improvement Guide to Personal and Business Success, 3rd ed. (self-pub., CreateSpace, 2013).

[43] Gary Allord, "Falciparum Malaria," *Vietnam Veterans Home Page*, rev. April 1, 1998, by DGS, http://www.vietvet.org/malaria.htm.

[44] "37 Venomous Vietnam Snakes—Dangerous and Some Deadly," *Thailand Snakes*, https://www.thailandsnakes.com/southeast-asia-venomous-snakes/Vietnam-snakes-venomous-dangerous/.

[45] Lillie Nyte, "Vietnamese Centipede/*Scolopendra subspinipes*," *ReptileApartment.com*, http://reptileapartment.com/Vietnamese-centipede-captive-care/.

[46] "Marines' Hymn," *Wikipedia*, https://en.wikipedia.org/wiki/Marines%27_Hymn.

[47] "Bell AH-1 Cobra," *Wikipedia*, https://en.wikipedia.org/wiki/Bell_AH-1_Cobra.

[48] "*Tarzan* (1966 TV Series)," *Wikipedia*, https://en.wikipedia.org/wiki/Tarzan_(1966_TV_series).

[49] John D. Dennison, "Glossary of Some of the Words Used during the Vietnam War," *1st Cav Medic*, http://www.1stcavmedic.com/glossary.html.

[50] John Stryker Meyer, "ST Idaho: Vietnam Recon Team Still MIA after 47 Years," *RallyPoint*, June 14, 2015,

https://www.rallypoint.com/status-updates/st-idaho-vietnam-recon-team-still-mia-after-47-years.

[51] Tom Pilsch, "Jolly Green 23 Found," January 23, 2003, www.tom.pilsch.com/AirOps/JG23-found.html.

[52] Grant Coates, "POW/MIA Affairs Committee Update January/February 2018," Vietnam Veterans of America, https://vva.org/programs/powmia/powmia-affairs-committee-update-januaryfebruary-2018/.

[53] "Vietnam War Casualties," *Vietnam War* (blog), October 4, 2009 (12:14 p.m.), http://vietnamwar-database.blogspot.com/2010/11/vietnam-war-casualties.html.

[54] Graham A. Cosmas and Terrence P. Murray, *U.S. Marines in Vietnam. Vietnamization and Redeployment, 1970–1971* (Washington, DC: History and Museums Division, Headquarters, US Marine Corps, 1986).

[55] Seth Marshall, "Tools of War: F-4 Phantom," *The Military Historian*, October 29, 2016, https://military-historian.squarespace.com/blog/2016/10/29/tools-of-war-f-4-phantom.

[56] Nikola Budanovic, "Liquid Fire—How Napalm Was Used in the Vietnam War," *War History Online* (blog), January 1, 2016, https://www.warhistoryonline.com/vietnam-war/history-napalm-vietnam-war.html.

[57] Nate Jones, "Nick Ut on His 'Napalm Girl' Photograph Years Later: 'Never in My Life Have I Seen What I Saw,'" *People*, June 8, 2014, https://people.com/celebrity/nick-ut-photographer-talks-kim-phuc-napalm-girl-photo-42-years-later/

[58] Arnold Blumberg, "Sapper Attack: The Elite North Vietnamese Units," *Vietnam Magazine,* February 1, 2017, http://www.historynet.com/sapper-attack-the-elite-north-vietnamese-units.htm.

[59] http://military.wikia.com/wiki/Vietnam_War_casualties.

---

60 "The VVA Self-Help Guide to Service-Connected Disability Compensation for Exposure to Agent Orange for Veterans and Their Families," Vietnam Veterans of America, May 2016, https://vva.org/wp-content/uploads/2014/12/AgentOrangeGuide.pdf.

61 Jack Keane, contributor interview, *Mornings with Maria Bartiromo*, January 11, 2018, Fox Business Network.

62 "Ho Chi Minh Trail," *United States History*, https://www.u-s-history.com/pages/h1875.html.

63 Norman B. Hannah, *The Key to Failure: Laos & the Vietnam War* (Lanham, MD: Madison Books, 1987), 34–35.

64 Ibid, 49.

65 *Encyclopedia Britannica Online*, s.v. "Frank Church," https://www.britannica.com/biography/Frank-Church.

66 Robert M. McNamara, *In Retrospect: The Tragedy and Lessons of Vietnam* (New York: Vintage Books, 1996).

67 Ibid, 101.

68 "Vietnam War U.S. Military Fatal Casualty Statistics," National Archives, https://www.archives.gov/research/military/vietnam-war/casualty-statistics.

69 Lance Morrow, introduction to *1968: The Year That Shaped a Generation; A Pictorial History*, ed. Donald Morrison (New York: Time, 1989).

70 "Pentagon Papers," *History.com*, https://www.history.com/topics/vietnam-war/pentagon-papers.

71 McNamara, xi.

72 "Tet Offensive," *History.com*, https://www.history.com/topics/vietnam-war/tet-offensive.

73 Santi, Suthinithet, "Land of a Million Bombs," Legacies of War, http://legaciesofwar.org/resources/books-documents/land-of-a-million-bombs/.

74 "Operation Rolling Thunder," *Wikipedia*, https://en.wikipedia.org/wiki/Operation_Rolling_Thunder.

[75] "List of Aircraft Losses of the Vietnam War," *Wikipedia*, https://en.wikipedia.org/wiki/List_of_aircraft_losses_of_the_Vietnam_War.
[76] Lewis Sorley, "The Abrams Tapes," *Vietnam Magazine*, December 2005, 36.
[77] McNamara, 267.
[78] http://legaciesofwar.org/resources/books-documents/land-of-a-million-bombs/.
[79] "Cambodian Campaign," Wikipedia, https://en.m.wikipedia.org/wiki/Cambodian_Campaign.
[80] Toum Bou Kim, "My Story," unpublished.
[81] "Cambodian Genocide," World without Genocide, http://worldwithoutgenocide.org/wwg/genocides-and-conflicts/cambodian-genocide.
[82] Jeff Lindsay, "Why Are the Hmong in America?" *JeffLindsay.com*, https://www.jefflindsay.com/hmong.shtml.
[83] http://worldwithoutgenocide.org/wwg/genocides-and-conflicts/cambodian-genocide.
[84] McNamara, 32.
[85] David H. Petraeus, "Korea, the Never-Again Club, and Indochina," Defense Technical Information Center, http://www.dtic.mil/dtic/tr/fulltext/u2/a518550.pdf.
[86] http://www.dtic.mil/dtic/tr/fulltext/u2/a518550.pdf.
[87] *Encyclopedia Britannica Online*, s.v. "Vietnam War," https://www.britannica.com/event/Vietnam-War.
[88] McNamara, 266.
[89] Barbara W. Tuchman, *The Guns of August* (Ballantine Books, 1994).
[90] "Khrushchev Loses His Cool," *Time.com*, http://content.time.com/time/specials/packages/article/0,28804,1843506_1843505_1843496,00.html
[91] "Nikita Khrushchev Quotes," WinWisdom Quotations, http://www.winwisdom.com/quotes/author/nikita-khrushchev.aspx

---

92 "When Bomb Shelters Were All the Rage," *Underground Bomb Shelter*, http://undergroundbombshelter.com/news/when-bomb-shelters-were-the-rage.htm.

93 "Eve of Destruction (Song)" *Wikipedia*, https://en.wikipedia.org/wiki/Eve_of_Destruction_(song).

94 Tuchman, *The Guns of August*, 275.

95 James Alexander Rentoul, "Hanoi's Triumph," *Time*, May 5, 1975.

96 Michael Dan Kellum, "The Leftwich Legacy," *Michaeldankellum.com*, http://www.michaeldankellum.com/index_htm_files/Shipmate-Article-on-Leftwich.pdf.

About the Author

Early in his adult life, David Gerhardt volunteered for the Marines and later for duty in Vietnam, where he served as a grenadier, awards writer, and combat squad leader. After his service in the marines, he became a businessman and entrepreneur, designing products that earned him patents in the U.S. and Canada. Previously, he authored the business book, "Communication Talks, B/S Walks." Dave and Connie live on a small horse farm in New Albany, Ohio.

Feedback

DavidGerhardtauthor

@DavidGE82006979

20504281R00161

Made in the USA
Middletown, DE
10 December 2018